Thriving

"It is so refreshing for someone to break through the paralyzing survival mentality and offer a strategy that enables us to thrive. The chapter 'You Are Here . . . and So Is God' alone is worth the price of the book. *Thriving* is a treasure map to abundant life."

Ken Davis, speaker, comedian, and award-winning author

"If you long to know who you are in Jesus Christ and you want to move forward in your life with purpose, courage, and intentionality, this book is for you. Nancy Grisham is a gifted communicator both on and off the platform, and her wisdom, biblical advice, and encouragement will capture your heart. *Thriving* will challenge you to renew your mind, ignite your passion, and engage in the adventure of a lifetime. I highly recommend this book for personal and for small group studies."

Carol Kent, author, *Between a Rock and a Grace Place*
and *When I Lay My Isaac Down*

"Through stories of her own hard times, Nancy shows us practically how to use the pain of our lives to drive us *to* the Lord and not *away* from Him. 'Real faith,' she writes, 'goes the distance with God, especially in rough terrain.' Now who wouldn't want to read, mark, inwardly digest, and apply the lessons of a book like this? I heartily recommend this book."

Jill Briscoe, author and minister, Elmbrook Church, Wisconsin

"Sometimes it's hard to know when we've settled for surviving. . . . Nancy has written a book that encourages us to take a hard look at the gap between surviving and thriving. Using life circumstances, effective practices, and out-of-the-box moments, the journey becomes an adventure in knowing a good God. And that changes everything."

Nancy Ortberg, author, *Looking for God: An Unexpected*
Journey through Tattoos, Tofu, and Pronouns

"Want to be spiritually encouraged, enlightened, and inspired? Then open this book! Let my friend Nancy Grisham lead you to a more authentic and vibrant faith in Christ."

Lee Strobel, bestselling author of *The Case for Christ*
and *The Case for Faith*

"I love this book. In each chapter I am challenged to embrace the Word of God and allow Scripture to serve as my daily GPS. Nancy Grisham writes with honesty and vulnerability about life's challenges and disappointments. She works through the process of embracing the Word over feelings and emotions. She gives directions on how to thrive when we find ourselves on a detour. Thriving is receiving from Jesus and surrendering to His love. Nancy is an example of a woman who has responded to His Word and is passionately in love with her Savior."

Linda Strom, author of *Karla Faye Tucker Set Free: Life and Faith on Death Row*; cofounder of Discipleship Unlimited prison ministry

"*Thriving* is one of those rare books that is filled with transparency, honesty, and encouragement. In these pages Nancy Grisham invites us to hear some of her own stories and the stories of her closest friends as she reminds us how life's sorrows and uncertainties can be met by God's faithfulness and goodness. This is a courageous and practical book, brimming with wisdom, which draws on the mature insights of Grisham's long walk with Christ."

Gary M. Burge, professor of New Testament, Wheaton College and Graduate School

"*Thriving* is a game changer. It will change the trajectory of your life as you are reminded of who God is and what He wants to do in, for, and through you. It is biblical, practical, and relevant for any person seeking to become all that God desires them to be. If you read one book this year, make it this one."

Steve Sonderman, associate pastor, Elmbrook Church; founder, No Regrets Men's Ministries

"We all know that Jesus said He came to give us 'abundant life' and that He would never call us to anything He wouldn't also equip us for. So why do we so often settle for less? How do we activate those promises in our everyday lives? Nancy Grisham's book takes us from surviving and striving to 'thriving.' It's your inheritance as a child of God—claim it!"

Terry Meeuwsen, co-host, *The 700 Club*, and founder/director, Orphan's Promise

"Nancy Grisham is a powerful communicator. She has written an engaging book that flows from her gritty experiences of life as well as her love for the Scriptures and the Lord Jesus Christ who is revealed therein. This volume will encourage Christians who face tough times and bring hope to folks who have not experienced a life-giving relationship with Jesus Christ."

Lyle W. Dorsett, PhD, Billy Graham Professor of Evangelism, Beeson Divinity School and Samford University

"Honest, refreshing, and insightful. Nancy offers more than a book. This is a journey of faith that will help you draw closer to God and encounter Jesus, as the Holy Spirit leads. If you want to thrive in your spiritual journey, read on!"

Kevin G. Harney, pastor of Shoreline Church and author of the Organic Outreach series and *Reckless Faith*

Thriving

TRUSTING GOD FOR
LIFE TO THE **FULLEST**

nancy grisham

BakerBooks
a division of Baker Publishing Group
Grand Rapids, Michigan

Published by Baker Books
a division of Baker Publishing Group
P.O. Box 6287, Grand Rapids, MI 49516-6287
www.bakerbooks.com

Printed in the United States of America

Library of Congress Cataloging-in-Publication Data is on file at the Library of Congress, Washington, DC.

ISBN 978-0-8010-1543-4

Unless otherwise indicated, Scripture quotations are from the New American Standard Bible®, copyright © 1960, 1962, 1963, 1968, 1971, 1972, 1973, 1975, 1977, 1995 by The Lockman Foundation. Used by permission.

Scripture quotations labeled KJV are from the King James Version of the Bible.

Scripture quotations labeled Message are from *The Message* by Eugene H. Peterson, copyright © 1993, 1994, 1995, 2000, 2001, 2002. Used by permission of NavPress Publishing Group. All rights reserved.

Scripture quotations labeled NIV are from the Holy Bible, New International Version®. NIV®. Copyright © 1973, 1978, 1984, 2011 by Biblica, Inc.™ Used by permission of Zondervan. All rights reserved worldwide. www.zondervan.com

Scripture quotations labeled NIV 1984 are from the Holy Bible, New International Version®. NIV®. Copyright © 1973, 1978, 1984 by Biblica, Inc.™ Used by permission of Zondervan. All rights reserved worldwide. www.zondervan.com

Scripture quotations labeled NKJV are from the New King James Version. Copyright © 1982 by Thomas Nelson, Inc. Used by permission. All rights reserved.

Scripture quotations labeled NLT are from the *Holy Bible*, New Living Translation, copyright © 1996, 2004, 2007 by Tyndale House Foundation. Used by permission of Tyndale House Publishers, Inc., Carol Stream, Illinois 60188. All rights reserved.

The internet addresses, email addresses, and phone numbers in this book are accurate at the time of publication. They are provided as a resource. Baker Publishing Group does not endorse them or vouch for their content or permanence.

13 14 15 16 17 18 19   7 6 5 4 3 2 1

In keeping with biblical principles of creation stewardship, Baker Publishing Group advocates the responsible use of our natural resources. As a member of the Green Press Initiative, our company uses recycled paper when possible. The text paper of this book is composed in part of post-consumer waste.

To Stuart and Jill Briscoe.

Thank you for your love for Jesus,
your humility in serving Him,
and your friendship to me along the way.
I thank God for you!

Contents

Acknowledgments

It is a great honor to say thank you to the people who walked with me along the journey of bringing this book into being.

My parents, David and Mildred Grisham, cast their anchor in God and wrapped us in love as they raised my sister Carole and me. They taught us a strong belief in Him, took us to church regularly, prayed at every meal, and built a foundation for strong character. Both my parents are now with Jesus—*I am so thankful for you!*

To Mark Mittelberg, Carol Kent, Lynda Elliott, Kevin Harney, Linda Strom, Jill and Stuart Briscoe, and Lyle Dorsett—thank you for sharing your experience as authors and for praying, reading, encouraging, and offering support as I wrote *Thriving*.

Thank you to Carl Turner, Dana Reaud, and Linda Strom for providing beautiful sanctuaries where I could get away to write. Thank you for the timely and generous gifts.

Thank you to my friends, including those above, who loved, prayed, read drafts, offered insight, and encouraged me along the way. Mary Perso, Wendie Connors, Francie Winslow, Barbara Findley, Terri Mitchell, Beth Gill, Lynda Elliott, Linda Strom, Nancy Morey, Ron and Terri Franks,

Suzanne Best, Marg Rehnberg, Beth Hadley, Sandra Hadley, Shelly Esser, Lynn Dugan, and Monica Lanham, you guys have been gold—*thank you*.

To my Livin' Ignited friends and to my former small group—thank you for your prayers and encouragement as I wrote this book. You guys are great.

Leanne Mellado and Dan Lovaglio of Willow Creek Community Church invited me to teach multiple series at the midweek classes. Those courses were the launching ground for this book—*thank you, Leanne and Dan*. And special thanks to all of you "Creekers" who participated in those classes!

Nancy Raney, vice president of publishing at the Willow Creek Association—thank for championing this book for publication! What an affirmation you were to me from that first meeting at Starbucks forward. Doug Yonamine, thanks for your valuable contract expertise in the process.

To the staff at Baker Publishing Group—it has been great to work with you! Chad Allen, my acquisitions editor, thank you for your input and for leading the way for *Thriving* at Baker. Wendy Wetzel, thank you for your expertise and kindness as my editor. To the marketing people, especially Mike Cook and Ruth Anderson, thank you for your ideas to help get *Thriving* into the hands of readers. Heather Brewer, thank you for your great work on designing the beautiful cover. To everyone on the Baker team who had a hand in *Thriving*, thank you for having your hearts turned toward Him and for doing what you do with excellence.

Some friends have played a special role in helping me grow in knowing and serving God. Your influence is woven throughout every chapter of this book: Jerry and Nancy Riddle, you taught me how to know Jesus better and grow through His Word; Suzanne Best, you helped me learn more about the Holy Spirit in my life; Lyle Dorsett, you taught me so much about His anointing; Stuart and Jill Briscoe, you taught me how to humbly serve Him and others in ministry; Lynda Elliott, you helped me navigate some tough times; Linda Strom, you've helped me learn to trust Jesus more; Mark Mittelberg, you've opened doors and continued to encourage me to write. I am so very grateful for each of you—*thank you.*

Most of all, my gratitude goes to Jesus. You are the life giver who empowers us to thrive, now and forever. *Thank you!*

Foreword

There is something deeply attractive about the title of this book. I think we all like the idea of *thriving*—but truth be told, most of us are focused on just *surviving*. Maybe you've noticed: living an authentic Christian life is not as easy as it used to be.

There was a time in the not-too-distant past when spiritual faithfulness seemed so much simpler. Much of our culture reflected—or at least respected—biblical values. Standing up for your faith evoked admiration from people all across the social spectrum, partly because they knew deep down that it was right and that they should be exhibiting the convictions they saw in you.

Times have changed. *People* have changed. They don't know what they used to know or respect what they used to respect. Our culture has become increasingly secular.

We're seeing what the Bible predicts when it warns about a time when people will "no longer listen to sound and wholesome teaching." Instead, "they will follow their own desires and will look for teachers who will tell them whatever their itching ears want to hear. They will reject the truth and chase after myths" (2 Tim. 4:3–4 NLT). They will be "boastful and proud, scoffing at God, disobedient to their parents, and ungrateful. They will consider nothing sacred" (2 Tim. 3:2 NLT). In addition, they will "say that evil is good and good is evil, that dark is light and light is dark, that bitter is sweet and sweet is bitter" (Isa. 5:20 NLT).

It's not a pretty picture, but it's an accurate one. This is a culture that pressures us to conform to its godless standards—and it sends us its messages relentlessly. Through television, the internet, movies, the news media, people at work and in the neighborhood, and sometimes even our own friends and family members, we're constantly nudged to lighten up and live like the rest of the world. And, ironically, the champions of "tolerance" are often the ones who least tolerate our Christian lifestyles—or us!

The pressure is not on us alone. Our kids go to schools where secular values triumph, political correctness is the norm, relativistic influences urge them to "find their own truth," and God is not welcome. Students are exposed daily to entertainment and influences that undermine biblical ideals. It seems that what's popular at every age level and in every corner of society today is antithetical to the teachings of Christ.

Add to all of this the constant busyness that keeps us on edge, the financial pressures of trying to make ends meet in an underperforming economy, and the internal temptations to stop serving God and other people. So often we're inclined to go our own way, do our own thing, and seek after whatever pleases and fulfills us.

Against such a backdrop it's difficult enough to *be* a Christian, let alone to genuinely thrive in your walk with Christ. Yet Nancy Grisham's wonderful book, *Thriving*, will help you do just that.

From the opening pages you'll sense what I've known for years: this woman is the real deal. She's an authentic Christian who has figured out (with God's help and the wisdom of His Word, she'll remind you) how to face life's most difficult challenges and not just endure, but overcome through the power of Christ. She vulnerably shares her own struggles along with the lessons she's learned, and she encourages us as readers to apply those lessons in the real-world situations we face each day. Over and over you'll find yourself saying, "Oh, I can relate to that story!" "Wow, that's good advice!" "Thanks, I needed that challenge!" And her chapter "Saying No to Fear" is pure gold—by itself it would easily be worth the price of the book.

I first met Nancy years ago when I was a pastor at Willow Creek Community Church in suburban Chicago. She showed up at the pilot presentation of a seminar I was developing with Lee Strobel—one that we later turned into the *Becoming a Contagious Christian* training course. Nancy immediately stood out in the class with her infectious faith. She went on to become an integral member of our church's outreach team. A few years later she moved to the Milwaukee area to become a leader at Stuart Briscoe's Elmbrook Church, where she started a ministry much like the one she'd been part of under my leadership at Willow Creek.

After that, Nancy moved back to Chicago to become a teacher at Wheaton College, where she helped students thrive in their faith and share it with others. She also played a key role at Wheaton's Billy Graham Center and spoke at Willow Creek conferences that I was facilitating. Ultimately, she established her own speaking and writing ministry called Livin' Ignited—a name that aptly describes the life she's lived ever since I first met her.

Oh, and somewhere in the midst of all that, Nancy managed to earn her doctorate at my alma mater, Trinity International University, in order to become better equipped to help churches minister to Christians and spiritual inquirers alike.

Nancy Grisham is a fired-up, sold-out, Spirit-filled, sincere, winsome, and wise follower of Christ. With humor and humility she teaches biblical principles that will help you grow in your faith. And she has somehow figured out how to wrap all of that up into this powerfully encouraging book, which I highly recommend reading and then passing on to others. In the process you'll be blessed, and you'll be a blessing to others. To quote the prophet Isaiah, you—and they—will "thrive like watered grass, like willows on a riverbank" (Isa. 44:4 NLT).

Mark Mittelberg, bestselling author
of *Becoming a Contagious Christian*
and *Confident Faith*

Introduction

Every day we face the challenge of living in a broken world. We want more than just to get through the difficulties. We want to thrive in life! This book is framed by the journey I took when life didn't deliver what I had expected. When challenges came my way, I wanted to learn how to experience life to the fullest in Christ—regardless of my circumstances. *Thriving* covers the key elements we need to know and trust God in order to experience all that He has promised us.

The book is divided into three sections: in part 1, "Knowing," we'll discover God's love, goodness, and presence. In part 2, "Overcoming," we'll explore renewing the mind, who we are in Him, and His provisions to overcome challenges. Finally, in part 3, "Thriving," we will gain knowledge of how to expect God's greatness, say no to fear, never quit, and never give up on God. Each section has vital information—keys for success in living life to the fullest.

Thriving will bring practical hope and encouragement through Christ for the best life available to you—now and later. You *can* enjoy knowing God, and you *can* experience life to the fullest in Christ. It's a white-knuckle adventure that awaits each one of us!

Part 1

Knowing

Leaning into the
God Who **Cares**

1

A Big Enough Love

Receiving God's Unfathomable Love

. . . .

I have loved you with an everlasting love.
Jeremiah 31:3

"It was stolen."

Those three words unveiled the beginning of a radical change in my life. My husband returned home one Sunday afternoon from an out-of-state golfing trip. He had been struggling with depression and hadn't been himself for a while. He said a golfing weekend with a buddy would give him a much-needed lift. He was a hard worker and weekends off were rare. I was excited for his chance to break out of the mundane for a little escape.

Even though we had been married almost eighteen years, I still looked forward to every time he walked through the door. However, this time, something was different. Very different. He arrived home in a taxi.

But he had left for the airport driving his SUV . . .
"Where's your car?"
"It was stolen."
There they were. Those three words. I was so disappointed for him. To think his golf weekend had ended like this. Then he told me the car had been stolen from a local Holiday Inn. I asked why it was there instead of at the airport. He sat down, lit a cigarette, and started to tell me the story.
But he hadn't smoked in years . . .
With those three words, his secret tryst with a childhood sweetheart began to unravel. There had been no golfing with a buddy. The police later found the SUV in an alley and it was repaired, but my life would never be the same. Just six weeks earlier, my husband had written me a passionate letter telling me how much he loved and valued me. But at that moment, I sat in our family room, raw with pain and anger.

We were both Christians; surely this wasn't happening. But it was. Within a few weeks, my husband decided to leave the marriage permanently. In the divorce, I got the house, the car, and our seventeen-year-old cat, Buster. Two weeks later, Buster died. Within months, my former husband remarried. In the coming years I would build a new life as a single—again.

Maybe you also have experienced a life-changing disappointment—through a broken relationship, the loss of a loved one, an illness, aging parents, job loss, foreclosure, or some other major upheaval. Sometimes these experiences mark us in ways we don't even understand. It's in these times of pain that our trust in God's love for us will be tested.

Life's disappointments have a way of spilling over into our relationship with God and coloring our perception of His love. They can drain the hope right out of our lives. However, it doesn't have to be that way. Those dark times can provide us with an opportunity to deepen our relationship with God and grow stronger in our faith. We can lean into the challenges instead of running away from them. When we live through tough times, we can come to know God better and experience his life-changing power in our lives.

The journey to thriving in life begins and moves forward by trusting God—secure in His love for us.

In the years after the divorce, I came to understand God's love for me in a greater way. Interestingly enough, the first year was the easiest because it was the most difficult. I *had* to depend totally on God to hold the pieces of my life together. My heart had been ripped apart by someone else's choices, but it was during this agony that God felt so very close to me. His love felt real, especially when I closed my eyes at night and talked with Him. I literally *felt* enveloped in God's love.

Sometimes God lets us enjoy an overwhelming sense of His presence. Those are powerful feelings. The time will come when those feelings go away because *feelings ebb and flow*. Does God love us any less when the tide changes? Has His love lifted? Have we done something that caused Him to pull back or reject us? These are the questions we silently struggle through when we don't *feel* God's love.

Let me make a bold, biblical declaration: God's love for us *never* changes. Never.

No matter what you have gone through in your life, no matter what you've done or what's been done to you, God loved you then and He loves you now. God will always love you.

Fickle Feelings

Maybe you're like me in that most days you don't walk around feeling God's love. Feelings change with diet, the weather, thoughts, amount of sleep, body chemistry, day of the week, and circumstances. When feelings tell us something other than the truth, we need to trust the truth and not our feelings. The only reliable trait about feelings is that given time they will change, because feelings are fickle.

Feelings don't change truth, which is to say they don't change God's love. He loves you whether you feel His love or not. When you've blown it badly, God loves you. When you've messed up again, God loves you. When you've thumbed your nose at Him, God loves you. When life disappoints you, God loves you. When people who should have loved you hurt you, God loves you. When you're not feeling the love from Him, your feelings haven't changed the truth—God loves you. God's love is bigger than your biggest feelings and your most painful situation.

One of the deadly weapons the enemy draws on us is when he tries to shoot down our confidence in God's love. The enemy tempts us with lies: "God doesn't love you. If God loves you, then why . . . ?" Too often we oblige the enemy by filling in the blank and running off in our reasoning because we're focused on how we feel.

I wrestled with this issue as I watched illness gradually strip the physical life from someone I dearly loved. I wanted to feel God's love, but I felt anger, disappointment, and grief. If I had believed my feelings, I would have reasoned that God didn't love me.

Our perception of God's love is shaded by so many factors. If life has been good, maybe we feel loved by Him. When life has been unfair and brutal, we may question His love. When we feel good about ourselves, we might think He loves us. If we've been hurt by people who should have loved and protected us, we often project their disfigured love onto God and we don't feel His love. There's a long list of hurdles that must be faced before simply believing the truth that *God loves me*.

There are seasons when God calls us to grow in knowing His love by faith, which will move us far beyond how we feel. For the rest of our lives we'll be growing in this process of trusting Him more and our feelings less. He wants us to know Him so well so that we can throw down our anchor into the truth of who He is, not into how we feel.

No matter what happens in your life, regardless of the pain you have endured, how people have wounded you, and even all the times that you've blown it, God *chooses* to love you.

An Unconventional Love

About once a year, I read through the first four books of the New Testament: Matthew, Mark, Luke, and John. In these books, we encounter grimy people with pains and foul diseases. They are drenched in sin and sorrow and disappointment. In story after story, these broken people make their way to a man in dusty sandals whose words launched creation and who holds the power of the universe by His word (Heb. 1:3). This man can drive out demons, resurrect dead bodies, heal terminal diseases, and forgive sinners. This man, Jesus, restored love to the world—to you and to me.

When you feel ashamed or sad or sinful, are you drawn to Jesus? People in the Gospels were drawn to Him because He offered a hope they had never before seen. He gave them help they couldn't find anywhere else. He ate with them, accepted them, healed them, freed them, and valued them beyond their wildest dreams. He washed dirty feet and forgave stained hearts. His love was unconventional. On the cross He would take on all of their sin and ours, die as our substitute, and defeat death itself.

When we meet Jesus, we meet love up close. From the very beginning of His public ministry, Jesus was love in the flesh—all God, all man, all power, all love. When He announced His work, He summed up His active mission of love very clearly:

> The Spirit of the Lord is on me,
>   because he has anointed me
>   to proclaim good news to the poor.
> He has sent me to proclaim freedom for the prisoners
>   and recovery of sight for the blind,
>   to set the oppressed free,
>   to proclaim the year of the Lord's favor. (Luke 4:18–19 NIV)

With these words, Jesus told us what His love would do for us. He spent the next three years putting His love into action.

"God anointed Him with the Holy Spirit and with power. . . . He went about doing good and healing all who were oppressed by the devil, for God was with Him" (Acts 10:38). Everywhere Jesus went, He loved people—everyone. He didn't come to judge or condemn them. He wasn't about loading them down with rules and regulations. Instead, through his life, death, and resurrection, He came to bring us goodness, pay the penalty for our sins, and set us free. Jesus extended the Father's love to all of us who would take Him up on His offer of freedom.

Jesus never met a person He didn't love. He looked past the social barriers, sin, inadequacies, and pride to see people with needs that only God could fill. His offer to each one was straightforward—love Himself.

Who are the kinds of people that Jesus loves?

The Marginalized

Have you ever felt "less than" other people, like you didn't quite measure up? One day a group of people came to Jesus. They weren't the movers and the shakers. They weren't the A-list people who everyone clamors to get near. In fact, they weren't even productive members of society. They were extra mouths to feed, they required extra resources, and it took time to care for them. They took a lot and had little to offer society. Some of Jesus's disciples thought that these people didn't warrant His attention, that they only got in the way of the important work He came to do. What did the disciples do? They tried to push them away. However, Jesus made it clear to everyone that He embraced those who were marginalized. He then blessed these children who had come to Him and declared their importance and worth to everyone. With this radical action, He put an exclamation point on the kind of people He welcomed to Himself—anyone who would come to Him as a little child (Mark 10:13–16).

Jesus's message was loud and clear: God's love is not reserved only for those who can benefit Him or society. His love is boundless, available to everyone who calls on Him—even those who have nothing to offer and who don't even try to pretend they do. People were simply drawn by the magnetism of this man Jesus. They came with reckless desire and were welcomed. Clearly, His was an all-encompassing love.

Maybe you've felt marginalized by the people who should have affirmed and valued you the most. Or you've felt sidelined because of your ethnicity, age, upbringing, gender, education, choice of sin, or _____ (fill in the blank). Maybe the sting of being passed over or looked down on has burned your soul. No matter what, God values you and loves you. You are so important to Jesus that *you* are the very person He came to reach. In His kingdom, love and acceptance can never be earned or deserved. Christ wants to *give* you an honored place with Him and put His blessing on your life. He gives you and me what we can never have without Him—real value based on *whose* we are, not on *what* we have to offer.

Condemned by the Self-Righteous

She was pulled from the bed of adultery and dragged into the public eye by arrogant religious men. They singled out her sin and dragged her before Jesus, demanding that He judge her. Imagine this traumatized woman, soaked in shame and trying to cover herself, dirty tears running down her face. They caught her in the act. Jewish law required she be stoned. They had her and wanted to use her to test Jesus's response. Never mind that it had taken two to commit adultery and that for whatever reason they didn't bring the man for judgment. Their message to Jesus was clear: "We dare you to give her what she deserves."

Initially, a smug self-righteousness hung in the air of her accusers. They were the religious, squeaky-clean rule keepers and proud of it. *They* didn't stoop to such a carnal activity as adultery. They were far too "religious" to commit such rancid sin. They were thought to be pillars in the church. If this story happened today, they could be the church leaders who paid their tithes, read their Bibles, obeyed the law, and said their prayers. People looked up to them. They were *not* her kind.

Jesus challenged these men: whoever among them had never sinned had permission to throw the first stone at the woman. Suddenly, they weren't feeling so self-righteous standing before Holiness. Not a stone was thrown. One by one, starting with the oldest, they walked away, acknowledging they weren't as good on the inside as they pretended to look on the outside. Jesus was left alone with this humiliated woman. He could have given her what she deserved in the Pharisees' eyes, but He extended mercy to her and told her not to sin anymore (John 8:1–11).

That day love had its way because "mercy triumphs over judgment" (James 2:13 NIV). However, only the adulteress received mercy. The accusers could have stayed, come to Jesus, and received mercy too. Instead, they missed the greatest opportunity of their lives. He was right before their eyes, and they missed Him. For some reason, they chose to walk away from Jesus instead of leaving their sin with Him.

When we look at ourselves, it's likely we aren't seeing the person Jesus sees. He knows our vulnerable places, our secret sins, and He loves us anyway. He offers mercy to us, too—to be our substitute, to take our sin, and to give us His righteousness (2 Cor. 5:21). And for our protection, He tells us not to go back to our old way of doing things.

The Pharisee

The people Jesus leveled His harshest words at were the Pharisees, the stringently religious leaders of the day, many of whom were hypocrites. They studied and outwardly kept the Jewish law to the finest detail. However, in their hearts they rejected God and His love.

One night, under the cloak of darkness, a Pharisee named Nicodemus came to Jesus. He was different because he had an open and seeking heart. He recognized that Jesus was from God. Jesus forthrightly taught him about the spiritual rebirth required to enter heaven: "Very truly I tell you, no one can see the kingdom of God unless they are born again" (John 3:3 NIV).

Jesus told Nicodemus how the spiritual rebirth takes place with these now familiar words, "For God so loved the world that he gave his one and only Son, that whoever believes in him shall not perish but have eternal life" (John 3:16 NIV). He made it clear that no one could ever be good enough, not even a Pharisee. The only way to God was—and still is—through trusting in Jesus. He said that whoever places faith in Him would experience spiritual rebirth—which results in a changed heart, freedom from bondage to sin, and eternal life in heaven.

After Jesus was crucified, it was Nicodemus who brought seventy-five pounds of myrrh and aloe to care for the body of Jesus at His burial (John 19:39). But this time he came in full view of the people. His openness to associate with Jesus, even in His death, indicates he had trusted Jesus as the only way to God. Just like Nicodemus, none of us can reach God on our own. We need a spiritual change from the inside out that only Jesus brings.

One Who Couldn't Get It Right

The woman couldn't make a marriage last if her life depended on it. She had tried and failed five times, so she had settled for a live-in arrangement. She wanted to be loved. She desperately needed someone to fill the cavern in her soul. However, each relationship ripped at her dignity and left her even more raw. Maybe she even felt like she had an invisible *L* stamped on her forehead for "loser."

She was a social outcast and avoided places where proper women gathered. But one day, as she was filling her water buckets when no one else was around, God came to her. In

His providence, her life intersected with Jesus. He offered her the drink that she had been looking for in all her relationships. Jesus had something she had never seen before—pure, unselfish love. That day, she accepted Jesus as the True Lover, and her life changed forever. The story didn't end at the well, though. In a culture that didn't accept the word of a woman—especially a divorced woman—God used her to spread the message of Jesus to her people (John 4:7–42)! No matter who you are or what you've done, God loves you and has greater plans for you.

Receiving God's Love

We can never stop God's love for us, but we can hinder our receiving of His love. Maybe you struggle sometimes with getting God's love settled into your life. Former hurts and losses may make it hard for you to believe that a loving God could have let your past happen to you. Maybe you're hurting right now and it's hard to imagine that a God who really cares for you would allow you to sit in this pain. Or maybe your life is better than you ever expected but something is still missing. Regardless of your particular situation, God loves you with an everlasting love (Jer. 31:3). This means that now and forever, God loves you. He tells us of His desire for us to know His love:

> that you, being rooted and grounded in love, may be able to comprehend with all the saints what is the breadth and length and height and depth, and to know the love of Christ which surpasses knowledge. (Eph. 3:17–19)

That's more than a truckload of love that God wants you and me to experience in our lives! It's a love so big, it can drive fear from your life and fill the deepest cracks of your soul with satisfaction. A love that rests in knowing you're His, secure in His care, wholeness, goodness, power, and restoration—His fullness. It is a love so powerful that it frees you to live in perfect security because *Love Himself loves you.*

One afternoon a friend was talking to me about how she came to know God's love. She had been through abuse during her childhood that caused a chasm between her identity and God's love for her. Later in life, she chose to walk in the opposite direction from God, and her soul was even more deeply wounded. She said,

> I didn't feel like I deserved the love of God, because I was in an immoral relationship. So I was trying to get right by not doing certain things. But I was trying to change in my power, not including God, because I didn't feel like I deserved Him. I was failing miserably. It was a cycle, a miserable cycle. I thought I had to get right first. I never felt like I was good enough, and I never felt like I deserved it. I got so frustrated. Finally, I came to the point that I was going to walk away from God completely and give up trying to live my life right. The thought of not having God in my life scared me, so I got on my knees one night and cried out to Him. All I heard in my heart was "I love you" . . . no judgment, all love. I then made up my mind to focus on His love first, and my behavior began to change.

My friend fought hard to believe she deserved God's love, but it wasn't working. Maybe you have questioned if you're good enough, or maybe you fear that you've gone too far away from God for Him to love you. The answer is simple—you aren't, never will be, can't be, and don't have to be good enough to deserve a love so big. Nobody is good enough, so we can relax and quit trying to earn God's love and approval. My friend went on to tell me,

> I have spent the majority of my life living out of insecurity. Because that was my foundation, it was easy for lies of the enemy to dominate my thought process. Finally, when I truly accepted that God loved me right where I was . . . insecure, sinful, and very alone . . . my whole life began to change. To

know that the God of the universe is *for* me has put a hope in my heart that I have never had before. His love has become my foundation. I look at life differently . . . I don't have to prove my worth to anyone . . . I am accepted and loved, and I'm being transformed by His goodness and love. There is no greater truth than to get how much God loves me, and out of that security, I am free!

Since none of us deserves God's love, how can we ever come to comprehend "the breadth and length and height and depth" of His love and "to know the love of Christ"? Even devoted Christ followers can struggle with truly believing and receiving God's love. We can believe we're forgiven and that we're going to heaven, and we can know in our heads that God loves us, yet we can miss fully receiving His love in our lives.

Many of us know about God's love in our minds. It's that eighteen-inch trip to the heart that often hits some road-blocks. You may have been betrayed, rejected, verbally abused, or painfully hurt by people who should have affirmed and loved you the most. Deep down, you may not feel too good about yourself. Underneath the thin veneer of a smile, you silently struggle to believe that you're totally accepted and loved by God. Or maybe your life has been just the opposite. Life has treated you well and you have been very fortunate. You feel good about yourself, and it's pretty easy to believe that God loves you.

It's important to realize that *both* of these views of God's love are self-based. Understanding the secret of receiving God's love begins with knowing that God's love is first about Him—His nature, His character. It reaches out to each of us regardless of how good or bad we act. His love is bigger than our behavior.

One morning, as I was praying with a friend, I became aware of how much more God deserved to be loved than how I loved Him. I began asking God to help me love Him more, to love Him the way He deserved to be loved. I thought I was doing some fine sounding praying. I remember thinking my friend was probably impressed with my prayer! Suddenly she interrupted our prayer time with these gentle words: "We never have anything to give to God but what we have received from Him. Let's stop right now and just receive the love of God."

My friend never opened her eyes. I, on the other hand, had both eyes open staring at her, a little embarrassed and stunned by her words. Then my friend began leading us in *receiving* from God: "O Father, thank You that You love us with an everlasting love. Thank You that as high as the heavens are above the earth, so great is Your love toward us. Lord, we receive Your love—we receive Your love . . ."

That morning my view of loving and being loved by God changed. Sometimes I put everything else on hold to stop and consciously receive God's love. I might say, "Father, thank You that You have loved me with an everlasting love. I receive Your love . . ."

One of the most well-known verses in the Bible about love is often skimmed over because we've heard it so often. However, the power held in that one verse is enough to change our eternity and our everyday alike. Think about each phrase as you read it.

> For God so loved the world,
> that He gave His only begotten Son,
> that whoever believes in Him
> shall not perish,
> but have eternal life. (John 3:16)

God gave Jesus "to restore love to the world."[1] Jesus is the beginning and the continuation of bringing God's love to us. He loves us so much that He died to pay the penalty for our sin. He does not want anyone to have to pay for sin when He has already paid the price for us. Jesus wants us to come to Him to receive forgiveness and the gift of eternal life—now *and* later.

What part of your soul needs to sit down and just be loved? Let Him be to you who He is . . . love. Where do you need to know God's love today? He is right there in your place of need. Where has life battered your soul? God wants to bring healing. Where have you substituted things, accomplishments, and people in place of God's love? None compares to Him. God's love doesn't mean that disappointments disappear on this side of eternity. It does mean that when pain comes, there's a love that gets us through the rough places to the other side of hope.

When I need to move toward recognizing and receiving God's love more, here are some things that have helped me.

- Replace old thoughts that say, "God doesn't love me" with true thoughts, "God loves me." When the old thought pops up, plug in the new thought.
- Thank Jesus that He loves you so much. Tell him you love Him.
- Talk to God like He loves you—He does!
- Find a Scripture passage on love that is especially meaningful to you. Talk to God about it. Ask Him to teach you more about His love.
- Look for God's love in practical ways. When something good happens, no matter how small, recognize it as an expression of God's love.
- Expect to experience God's love in practical ways.
- Give God's love to other people without expecting their love in return.

God has poured out His love into our hearts by His Holy Spirit (Rom. 5:5). He wants us to simply become good receivers. Every football player knows what it means to be a good receiver. You open up your hands to the ball, grab it, run with it, and you don't let go until the whistle is blown. God's love has come straight to you and me. He never misses His intended receiver. Never. Trust Him that His love is so big that you will not miss it. Open wide and receive.

God's Love and Loving Plan

Love is an integral part of God's character. As A. W. Tozer said, "The words 'God is love' mean that love is an essential attribute of God."[2] However, He is also holy, just, all-knowing, all-powerful, sovereign, and so much more!

Love envelops all of what God does. He can never act outside of love, because it's woven throughout His nature. When we start to define God's love by our own or other people's lives, circumstances, thoughts, or feelings, there isn't enough room for Him to be who He really is. His compassion and love are too big to fit into our finite understanding.

When we see the way Jesus loves people, we see the Father's love for us. He is the perfect image of God. Only in truly knowing Christ are we released from the tyranny of thinking that we could ever earn or deserve such an extravagant love.

Jesus told His friends, "Greater love has no one than this, that one lay down his life for his friends" (John 15:13). He then demonstrated His love for them—and for you and me—by willingly giving His life on the cross and defeating death on our behalf. Jesus was all God and all man. He made a way for us to be friends with the holy God through faith in Him. We will never deserve such a friendship, but the one who loves us most offers it to us freely. Our role is to receive both the gift and the Giver.

. . . **Taking the Next Step** . . . .

Think about It

In this chapter we've focused on how we can know God's love through Christ, even when we may not *feel* His love. Many factors can influence our perception of His love. Take a few minutes to reflect on these questions to help you process your understanding and reception of God's love.

1. How has a person, event, Scripture passage, or something else helped you become more aware of God's love for you?
2. In what ways have circumstances helped to shape your perception of God's love?
3. In what ways does Jesus help reveal God's love to you?
4. What hinders you from being a better receiver of God's love in your life?
5. How might your confidence in God's love for you affect your relationship with Him? With others? With yourself?

Put It into Action

Scripture takes us to God and anchors us in His truth that never changes. The truth is—*God loves you!*

> The LORD your God is with you,
>   he is mighty to save.
> He will take great delight in you;
>   he will quiet you with his love,
>   he will rejoice over you with singing. (Zephaniah 3:17 NIV 1984)

Write out the above verse and keep it with you this week. Read and reflect on it several times a day. Each time you read the verse:

1. *Enjoy* what God is saying to you,
2. *Thank* Him for loving you, and
3. *Receive* His love for you.

The Goodness of God

Trusting God When the Going Gets Tough

. . . .

> I remain confident of this:
> I will see the goodness of the LORD
> in the land of the living.
>
> Psalm 27:13 NIV

Late one afternoon, I received a phone call that launched my wheels airborne: "Melissa's got stage-four colon cancer." Surely it couldn't be true. Melissa, my precious niece, was a vivacious thirty-four-year-old, a wife, a mother of four, and a Christ follower. Nothing like this happens in our family!

For the next nine months, we walked through that shadowed valley with Melissa. The doctors unleashed every possible treatment on her body. We prayed for healing, cried out to God, and imperfectly trusted Him. The day we moved Melissa to hospice, family and friends walked along behind her hospital bed as it wound through the long corridors of the medical center. I remember thinking it felt like we were in a New Orleans funeral procession, marching along to a silent dirge, but Melissa was still alive.

God healed Melissa—on the other side of eternity. When her wonderful husband, Brian, told the children, their seven-year-old daughter asked, "Who's going to teach me to be a big girl?" The world doesn't have a safety net for that kind of loss.

Two weeks before Melissa died, her brother's wife, Jill, had been diagnosed with leukemia. Jill was assigned the room across the hall from Melissa. We were in another savage war for a vibrant young life. Twenty-four months later we lost the battle again. I spoke at Jill's funeral, thankful that she also knew Christ. The following year I said an agonizing good-bye to my mother. Cancer had stripped the life from her body. Heaven was a little fuller, but my heart had a huge empty place.

During those brutal months, I asked God the same gut-wrenching questions most of us ask when life bludgeons us. *Why? With one word You could heal—one word. Jesus, would You please say that word? If it takes faith to bring healing and none of us has enough, would You please take all our little faiths, add them together, and in Your mercy HEAL?*

Maybe you've been through difficulties that have caused you to question God. Maybe there have been times in your life when you've felt like I did. For the next few months, I didn't feel much beyond deeply numbing disappointment and loss. Although I absolutely believed that God is good and that His desire is life and health, I honestly *felt* like He could and should have done a lot better for us. Along with one well-known author, I *felt* "that God should somehow 'do a better job' of running the world."[1] Maybe you've felt as if God has let you down in some way too. You now find yourself blaming Him and questioning His nature.

Sometimes our emotions are louder than our faith. We need to come to grips with the truth of where we are before we can move forward to where we need to be. How do we regain our bearings when the wind has been knocked out of our hope and our faith is wobbling? What do we do when something has shifted on the inside and we feel like God didn't come through for us? It does not have to be a long road back to trust in God. It does, however, have to be the right road, and that road begins by leaning into the absolute goodness of God.

The "If God . . ." Grid

Every time trouble slams us against the wall, the temptation to doubt God is crouching in the shadows. When we're discouraged, we're tempted to run our circumstances through the "If God . . ." grid. When we do this, we sift God and our problems through the framework of our limited understanding. We test God and come to a self-defined truth that accuses God of not being good.

If God is good . . .

Why did He let this happen?

Why doesn't He change my circumstances?

Why didn't He protect my family from this tragedy?

Why doesn't He do something to help me?

You could add your own questions to the list. If circumstances are bad, we're tempted to weigh God's character in the balance of our mind. However, our understanding is so finite. When our lives are tossed into chaos, doubt is coiled to strike at our faith. Its venom delivers a concentrated dose of distortion and deception. Doubt has been with us since Eden when the enemy hissed to the woman, "Indeed, has God said, 'You shall not eat from any tree of the garden'?" (Gen.

3:1). As Ruth Paxson said, "A subtle insinuation is couched in these words which was intended by the tempter to arouse suspicion of God's goodness."[2] The fact is we don't need the answers to our questions as much as we need confidence in God—that He really is good.

When we are wrestling with questions, the place to take them is straight to truth Himself, Jesus. Denying that we have these questions only gives them more power to spread underground into our lives. When we're honest with God, we can bring our doubts and questions to Him, and then He can help us.

We can look in the Psalms at how people spilled their thoughts and emotions out to God. They told Him what they thought, how they felt, and what they needed. He wants us to interact and relate with Him. We can tell Him that we are in pain, that we're confused, angry, and disappointed. He knows what's on the inside of us, and He wants *us* to see what's there. When we're honest, we are on our way to a better understanding of knowing Him. As we come to know Him better, the "If God . . ." grid begins to disappear in exchange for trusting Him. We can begin to view life through God's perspective instead of viewing God through our pinhole perspective.

We've all experienced pain. Some people grow stronger through the experience while others drown in despair. We've all struggled with the undertow of doubt. Sometimes we've shouted out, lashed out, and acted out. On really dark days we've wondered if there even is a God and if there's a point to this whole thing called life. Our image of God has become distorted by looking at Him through the lens of circumstances. That's like looking at God through the wrong end of the binoculars. God is *so much bigger* than He appears in our natural minds.

When life hurts, it's sometimes hard to separate our circumstances from the character of God. In our pain, disappointment, and anger we are tempted to blame Him. When we blame Him for our problems, our disappointment overshadows our understanding of Him. But as we learn to run to God, it stops the damage from spreading and begins restoration.

Trouble can destroy us—but it doesn't have to. When it's handled poorly, it can shrivel and embitter our souls. However, God can turn what the enemy meant for evil and use it for our good (Gen. 50:20). God wants us to know Him so well that we can anchor our confidence in Him. Our adversary, Satan, is always looking to take someone down. He has a threefold mission in our lives to steal, kill, and destroy (John 10:10). He will use life's disappointments to try to accomplish that mission. However, God is so much greater. His goal is to help us overcome in the midst of even the worst problems. Even when everything else seems against you, God is for you (Ps. 56:9). Run to Him for help!

Separating Circumstances from God's Character

A few years before Melissa died, I was going through a really difficult season in life. I was on the phone talking to a friend about it. She was an extremely merciful person, and I felt certain she would say, "There, there. You're such a trooper. You've served God so faithfully. This isn't fair." However, her words came from a totally different direction.

She abruptly stopped me mid-whine and said, "This is what you're really asking, 'Is God good?' If you don't get that question settled, you're never going to be able to trust Him, because if you don't believe that God *is* good, you *can't* trust Him." Thank God for friends who speak truth in love!

She was right. I was off course. I absolutely knew God was good. However, I had let my eyes wander over to my circumstances. Reason and emotion had locked my focus on what was happening in my life. Pretty soon my perspective of God was slightly distorted. At the core of my complaining was the underlying accusation, "God, You're not working things out for my good in the way I think You should be." I had set myself up as knowing and doing better than God. How ridiculous! I'd fallen prey to doubting the character of God.

When I got off the phone, God and I did some serious business. My part was choosing to run to God for help. His part was loving me, forgiving me, dusting me off, and setting me on the right course again. He helped me refocus and believe that regardless of what was happening in my life, He *is* good. In all circumstances, in every way, forever God is good. Settled. That day I made a renewed decision of faith based on the true character of God.

Maybe you've silently (or not so silently) shaken your fist at God. It's been said that "it's better to shake a fist than turn tail." After all, it seems logical to think that if He is all-powerful and all-good, which He is, then He needs to intervene and make wrong things right—*now*.

Sometimes in our misguided reasoning we feel like we've been trying to do our part; not perfectly of course, but then we're not God. We quietly think that He doesn't seem to be holding up His end of the deal. In other words, "If the problem's not me, it must be You." When this happens we need to hit the brakes, back up, and get our thinking in line with the truth. Just as Satan accuses us before God (Rev. 12:10), he also accuses God before us. The enemy lies. Here's the truth as laid out from Genesis to Revelation: *God is good, He loves you, and He is for you.* He's the One who's working to help you get through the trouble. Anything less than the truth about Him is a lie. Don't fall for the enemy's lies!

There have been a lot of excellent materials written about the goodness of God in the badness of life. Knowing and believing His goodness are foundational. At some point nearly all of us will grapple with this issue. We live in a broken world where 9/11 happens, where Auschwitz happens, where tsunamis hit and hundreds of thousands die, where cancer hits, where a father of five is paralyzed by a drunk driver, where parents divorce, and where innocent children are slaughtered. Based on the truth of the Bible, I still choose to believe the goodness of God. However, this doesn't mean that I have reconciled the tension I feel. It means that my tension and faith can coexist, with my confidence in God being the greater of the two.

God's Goodness

When life hits the fan and normal flies to pieces, nuzzling up to God would not be the first response for many people. Many people isolate themselves, bury themselves in work, or go to friends or self-help books as a first resort. However, confidence in God grows by knowing Him through the Bible. As A. W. Tozer said, "That God is good is taught or implied on every page of the Bible and must be received as an article of faith as impregnable as the throne of God. It is a foundation stone for all sound thought about God."[3]

The psalmist David knew struggle, he knew pain, but most of all he knew and trusted God and His goodness—all the while feeling the same emotions we feel.

In Psalm 103, David lists an array of amazing things God had given him. As we will see, the list goes on and on! We don't know what David was feeling that day. However, we do know that he *tells* himself what to do: "Bless the LORD, O my soul, and forget none of His benefits" (Ps. 103:2). David tells his soul, "You *will* bless the Lord!" When we don't know what to do, the best thing is to put our focus on God and *tell* our soul the right thing to do. It's always right to remember how good God has been to us.

David sets a great example for us because he's so raw and real with God. He starts some of the psalms by crying out to God about the problem. He tells God exactly how he feels, sharing his anger, disappointments, discouragement, and pain. Most of the time, he then shifts gears and starts to talk about God's character and promises. By the end of his prayer, he has often left the problem behind and is worshiping God.

David establishes a pattern for us: go to God, tell Him the problem, and remember His greatness. We have a choice to bow to Him instead of to our problems and feelings. Remembering God's goodness is fuel for the power of worship. In Psalm 103 and many other psalms, David makes the choice to begin and continue in worship, grateful for God's goodness to him.

All the benefits David writes about in Psalm 103 are the exact benefits that God has given you and me in Christ. They are spiritual benefits that are meant to become realities in our daily lives. They are for now *and* they are eternal.

Circumstances come and go; however, God's benefits to you and me are forever. He wants us to recognize and receive them. Every time I read Psalm 103, I'm struck by the practical goodness of God in our lives.

> Who pardons all your iniquities,
> Who heals all your diseases;
> Who redeems your life from the pit,
> Who crowns you with lovingkindness and
>   compassion;
> Who satisfies your years with good things,
> So that your youth is renewed like the eagle.
>
> The LORD performs righteous deeds
> And judgments for all who are oppressed. . . .
> The LORD is compassionate and gracious,
> Slow to anger and abounding in lovingkindness. . . .
>
> For as high as the heavens are above the earth,
> So great is His lovingkindness toward those who fear
>   Him.
> As far as the east is from the west,
> So far has He removed our transgressions from us.
> Just as a father has compassion on his children,
> So the LORD has compassion on those who fear Him.

For He Himself knows our frame;
He is mindful that we are but dust. . . .

But the lovingkindness of the LORD is from everlast-
    ing to everlasting on those who fear Him,
And His righteousness to children's children,
To those who keep His covenant
And remember His precepts to do them.

The LORD has established His throne in the heavens,
And His sovereignty rules over all. (vv. 3–8, 11–14,
    17–19)

Which of these benefits do you need most in your life right
now? They all belong to you in Christ. Take the time to go
back through the list and personalize each benefit. "God, You
pardon all my iniquities. Thank You that You have forgiven
all of my sins." That one verse changes everything! Only
God can give this level of full and complete forgiveness in
the spiritual realm—and He gives it to you and me, because
He is good. When I come to "who heals all your diseases,"
I thank Him, even in the tension of life's disappointments.

God has so much good available for you. His love for you
is so great that He doesn't want you to leave anything He
has given you on the table. He wants you to enjoy the full
benefit of all His goodness. Everything on David's list is on
your list. Those benefits are a *fact* for you whether you feel
them or not. Write your name in there, thank God, receive,
and celebrate how good He is to you. Whether your happenings are happy or hard, God offers all His goodness to you,
all the time in Christ. He is such a good God!

One Sunday as I was about to take communion, I came
into a fresh awareness of what Jesus had done when He died
for my sins and rose from the grave. It hit me like a spiritual
freight train—the bread and the wine, the body and the blood
of Jesus were for *me*. He had snatched *me* out of the pit of
hell and given *me* His real life. Good news indeed! All of the

things that I had ever done wrong had been wiped off the board—forgiven. I remember thinking, "God, if You never did another thing for me the rest of my life, that's enough."

Later, I was talking to the pastor and told him, "I realized during communion if Jesus never did another thing for me, what He did on the cross was enough." He looked at me and said, "But He didn't stop there." I've thought about that so many times over the years. Jesus didn't stop at just forgiving us and snatching our lives from the pit. Yes, that would have been enough, but He offers so much more than that. Jesus came to give us life *and* to give us life more abundantly (John 10:10). He took our sin, died as our substitute, rose from the dead, *and* sent His Holy Spirit to help us every day. He gave us every spiritual blessing in the heavenly places, *and* He raised us up to sit at His right hand, in both the sweet now *and* later (Eph. 1:3; 2:6). Jesus opened up a whole new extraordinary way of living beyond our comprehension. Talk about the good life! It is found in Christ Jesus *now*—by faith.

Every day God radically gives to us out of His love and goodness. It's a life-altering truth—*God is good and He loves you.* He sees you right where you are, knows you, and totally loves you. He doesn't give you a barely-get-by life so you can eke along on your way to heaven. He offers you a more-than-enough, extraordinary life right now.

God's goodness and love extends to every area of our lives. Several years ago a friend invited me to join her as she spoke at a retreat on the shores of a large bay on the Great Lakes. While teaching one evening, she talked about God giving us a visual illustration in Psalm 103 of the vastness of His love: "For as high as the heavens are above the earth, so great is His lovingkindness toward those who fear Him" (Ps. 103:11).

After the session I asked her if she wanted to go to the show. She gave me a bewildered look. I explained that I meant God's show up in the heavens. We made our way down to the lake to a very long dock. We went to opposite ends of it, laid back, and looked up at brilliant stars. We stayed there in silence looking at the stars and the visual illustration of the depth and height of God's love for us.

Sometimes we're unaware of all the good that is in our lives because we're focusing on our smallness or we're locked into the negative. Maybe we need to go out on a dark night, look up at the stars, and be reminded of God's love. I heard it said somewhere, if you ever think there's not much good happening in your life, consider what you would miss if everything good were suddenly gone tomorrow. Then start thanking God for each one of the things you would miss. I would miss everything from the people I love to my first cup of coffee in the morning, and most all the things in between. When we flip the switch off the negative and onto the positive, we suddenly have a fresh perspective. We can't even take a gulp of air but for the goodness of God who gave us spring-back lungs!

By God's grace, good can be happening *in* us even when trouble is happening *to* us. God's goodness is not limited by our feelings or our happenings. God can give us the help we need right where it's needed. He doesn't always intervene to change immediate circumstances, although sometimes He does change them. However, when everything in our lives is given over to Him, He will use even the bad for good.

God Gives Good Not Evil

Recently a friend who was going through breast cancer told me how she has leaned into God like never before. She said that she's experiencing Jesus in a whole new way. We had dinner together, and she was the most vibrant I've ever seen her. She shared, "For the first time in my life I'm seeing Jesus as my warrior. It seems at every turn that He has been making Himself known to me as the one who is fighting for me and being my champion in the battle." I sat there amazed at the grace that was on her. She was powerfully experiencing God during the hardest time of her life. When we go through the fire, He is always right there with us to give us His strength, peace, and joy—to give us Himself.

Maybe you've heard well-meaning people say, "God caused this [insert something horrid] to teach me a lesson." What kind of holy God would He be if He went around doing wrong? Evil and its consequences come from a lot of different avenues because we live in a broken world. However, God doesn't broker evil in our lives. "The thief comes only to steal and kill and destroy; I came that they may have life, and have it abundantly" (John 10:10). Run your circumstances through the grid of that verse. The thief is Satan. God is working in our lives to bring about life to the fullest—in, through, and even in spite of the destruction the enemy hurls against us.

When evil happens, God can ultimately take what was meant for destruction and turn it for good. He doesn't bring evil, but because of His power and redemptive work, He is not limited by it. He never wastes pain. "And we know that all things work together for good to those who love God, to those who are the called according to His purpose" (Rom. 8:28 NKJV). His goodness is not limited, except for where we limit Him in our lives. If we have a true picture of God in our minds, it will expose the deception when we accuse Him of wrong motives and actions.

When God created the world, He made it perfect with no evil. That was God's design. When he looked at His work, He repeatedly said, "It is good." He planned for us to live and enjoy paradise in perfect relationship with Him. Then the enemy deceived Eve into thinking maybe God wasn't totally good, maybe there was something better, maybe He was keeping something good from her. Eve acted on that doubt and disobeyed God. Adam was close behind and willfully made the same choice. At that point, rebellion entered humanity, and Satan, the originator of evil, unleashed all manner of evil into this world.

Jesus came to give us life to the fullest. However, He said, "In this world you will have trouble" (John 16:33 NIV). What we all wish He had said was, "If you trust Me all your troubles will be over." Instead He told us that no one takes a pass on trouble in this broken world. Why? Because the whole world lies in the power of the devil and his mission is to steal, kill, and destroy.

Years ago I read that one day Jesus will not only deliver us from the *penalty* and the *power* of sin (which He's already done), but eventually He will deliver us from the *presence* of sin. That stuck with me because there is a presence of sin all around us. However, a time is coming when Jesus will return, take His people to heaven, and make all things right. No more stress, anxiety, disappointment, pain, illness, or death. No more presence of evil . . . only all good, all the time. But until then the presence of evil is all around us.

Once when some followers turned away from Jesus, He asked His remaining disciples if they also wanted to leave Him. Peter said, "Lord, to whom shall we go? You have words of eternal life. We have believed and have come to know that You are the Holy One of God" (John 6:68–69). Peter had a relationship with Jesus that enabled him to trust Him. When we don't understand life, it helps to remember that the only one who has the *words* of eternal life is the same one who *gives* eternal life. The trouble we have now is temporary—it has an expiration date.

We all get hit with the flying debris of a broken world. I'm convinced that God protects us far beyond our awareness of His intervention. He has angels who are dispatched to guard and deliver us (Ps. 91:11). His goodness shields us from so much every time we get in the car and drive down the interstate. However, there remains a nebulous trouble in this world that Jesus said would come to everyone. The psalmist got it right when he said, "I would have lost heart, unless I had believed that I would see the goodness of the LORD in the land of the living" (Psalm 27:13 NKJV). God's will is for us to *see* His goodness in *this* life.

Trusting in the Tough Times

Our relationship with Christ can be strong enough to trust Him when life hurts. If God is only as big as our mind's ability to understand Him, He would be no greater than our human mind. Who would want to rely on that tiny god? However, many people do trust in just such a god—one they've made in their own image of understanding. We want, need, and *have* a much bigger God.

When we live by what we see, feel, hear, touch, and think, we are limited to the natural realm. Within those limitations we will get caught in a vortex of expectation, disappointment, and doubt. We're like spiritual yo-yos, going up, down, and all around. We can overcome this downward spin by trusting God. As we get closer to the one who loves us, especially during times of difficulty, He can make Himself known in ways that we have never yet experienced. "God is our refuge and strength, a very present help in trouble" (Ps. 46:1). Our role is to reach out to Him and receive Him.

There is life-giving power and hope that are unleashed when we put our focus on God instead of on our problems. There is also a negative power when we focus on our problems; it's called *worry*. It's a form of fear, and it will drain the joy and strength right out of our lives. However, we can look to God for who He is, what He does, and what He gives. He will change us on the inside and plant faith firmly in our lives.

While we're in the grip of trouble, our confidence in God's goodness will be tested. Emotions may scream at us, and reason can rant a seemingly logical twist of the truth. However, ultimately we decide where we put our faith—we *choose* to trust in *knowing* that God is good. Anything else will eventually come crashing down around us. Trusting in God's goodness raises us toward His perspective of power, possibility, and life to the fullest—regardless of our circumstances.

.... Taking the **Next Step** . . . .

Think about It

We've been looking at having absolute confidence in God's goodness. This truth is pivotal in trusting God, especially when times are tough, because faith is anchored in the good character of God. Thoughtfully respond to these questions as you consider His goodness and how it relates to your life.

1. How might circumstances in your life have influenced your confidence or lack of confidence in God's goodness?
2. If all goodness, which only comes from God, were suddenly pulled from the earth today, how might your life be different?
3. Read Psalm 103 again. As a Christian, which of these benefits are you especially thankful for today and why?
4. Which of the benefits listed in Psalm 103 do you need to receive more fully into your life?
5. In what ways are you extending God's goodness to the people in your life?

Put It into Action

Give thanks to the LORD, for He is good. (Ps. 118:1)

Every morning this week, before your feet even hit the floor, thank God for ten (yes, ten!) of the good things in your life.

Each night this week, when your head hits the pillow, thank God for ten (yes, another ten!) good things from your day.

You Are Here . . .
and So Is God

Become Present in the Presence of God

. . . .

> In Your presence is fullness of joy;
> In Your right hand there are pleasures forever.
>
> Psalm 16:11

Almost every year Mary, one of my closest friends, and I take a weekend road trip to Door County, Wisconsin, the "Cape Cod of the Midwest." It's a great place to hike, ride bikes, watch sunsets, drink coffee, and eat some serious cherry pie.

On one trip we were driving down a country road and saw a small sign with the words "The Clearing." Curious, we turned into the narrow drive that was lined with trees and overgrown prairie grasses. Finally we came to a large clearing, but it was the parking lot. A little disappointed, we parked the car and walked up to a small stone house that was surrounded with prairie flowers.

We arrived just in time to join a walking tour of "The Clearing." About a hundred yards from the house, we came to a large clearing with a fire pit encircled by stone seating. The guide waited for us to get settled. A little skeptical, I waited for something weird to happen. Instead, the guide started telling us the story of Jens Jenson, one of America's foremost landscape architects, who had designed The Clearing's acres of meadows and forest along the shoreline.

"A lot of people come here expecting to find a large clearing in the woods. However, that wasn't the clearing Jenson envisioned. He wanted a place where people could come away and *clear their heads* from the stress of modern life and reconnect with nature." I suddenly realized that I had fallen into the same mindset. Sometimes we can't see the clearing through the trees.

Our little band of adventurers left the fire pit and followed the guide through the forest, toward the shoreline of Green Bay. The path was craggy, with gnarly roots and tree trunks that made for slow navigation. I was beginning to feel really irritated that the path was so unkempt and slow. Surely they could have removed some of the bigger roots and trunks! Almost simultaneously the guide turned around and said, "One of the things that Jenson specifically designed was that the pathways be rough, with turns and roots to force people to slow down and experience nature." What a surprise to realize that I was in lockstep with the hurry-up mentality. I needed to slow down.

I was about to miss the experience of The Clearing because I like to go fast, get where I'm going, and then go somewhere else. Jenson had people like me, and maybe you, in mind when he designed this nature sanctuary.

When it comes to slowing down and being present with God, it may seem easier to just keep going. If we continue the fast path, one day we'll sense that gnawing feeling on the inside that something is missing. Our soul becomes dull, and we realize that we're dragging through life like a slug on sand. The pathway is overgrown, and hope has turned a sullen gray.

We feel distant from God, as though He left the building and turned off the lights. Only we're the ones who've turned away from our awareness of Him.

Maybe you've also had times when you felt like God was so present that He was almost tangible. You felt loved, courageous, and powerful. You knew He is real, and you felt especially close to Him. Those are powerful, rich, feel-good kinds of times. However, regardless of how you feel or don't feel, God is *always* present.

We all need a place on the inside where we can clear our heads and experience the presence of God. He invites us to slow down and live in the constant awareness of His Spirit.

You Are Here . . .

A while back my neighbor, Vicki, and I loaded up our camera gear and drove to a place called Starved Rock to photograph a small waterfall ("small" is the only kind of waterfall we have in Illinois!). We both enjoy photography, so we left at 5:30 a.m. and filled up on coffee for the two-hour drive to the trailhead. The entry to the trail had a large map that was clearly marked "You are here." We studied the map, got our bearings, and took off down the trail. After a long, hot, muggy hike, we found the waterfall, set up our equipment, and took some photos.

Later I got to thinking about the words on the map: "You are here." If we could look at a map of God's presence in relationship to where we are at this precise moment, it would read, "You are here . . . and so is God."

God is everywhere. David asked if there was anywhere he could go where God wouldn't be. He concluded that even in the far distance and in the darkness, God is always there (Ps. 139:7–8). As A. W. Tozer once wrote, "Wherever we are, God is here."[1] While the Spirit of God is everywhere, He has uniquely given His Spirit to live in every Christ follower.

Before Jesus left earth, He told His disciples that it was better for them that He went away because He would send them a helper (John 16:7). He promised to send His Spirit who would help and always be with His followers.

In every portion of every second, God is with us. He's in the family room, at the office, on the golf course. He's with you while you're mowing the yard, digging in the flowerbed, or even when you're having a pity party. God is always *here*. There is absolutely nowhere you and I can go, nothing we can do, but that God's presence isn't there too. While *we* may vacillate in and out of our awareness of Him, *He* never leaves us (Heb. 13:5).

It's so good when we can sense God's presence, but maybe you're like me in that you usually don't *feel* the presence of God in your life. It's important to remember that God is Spirit, and our feelings swim in the natural realm. Regardless of how we feel, we can trust Him to be true to His Word when He says He's *always* with us. As I've heard author Jill Briscoe say, "When you can't feel Him with your feelings, feel Him with your faith!"

God Wants Us to *Enjoy* His Presence

When I was teaching at a Christian college, I had a conversation with a colleague, Dr. Sam Storms, who had written a book about enjoying God and knowing that He enjoys us. That talk had a profound influence on me. We often think about believing, obeying, hearing, serving, and loving God. How often do we hear about enjoying Him? God wants us to enjoy His presence in the routine rhythms of life, confident that He enjoys us! When we turn our attention to Him, He enables us to live with our minds cleared of the things that distract us from Him. God wants us to enjoy being present with Him in our day-to-day activities, realizing that He is right here with us—enjoying us. The psalmist puts it this way:

> You make known to me the path of life;
>   you will fill me with *joy in your presence*,
>   with eternal pleasures at your right hand. (Ps.
>   16:11 NIV, emphasis added)

Life is a pathway, not a freeway, when it takes place in the awareness of God's presence. It is a pathway that turns drudgery into a rich journey filled with gratitude for who He is and what He has done for us. The Message puts it this way:

> I'm happy from the inside out,
>   and from the outside in, I'm firmly formed.
> You canceled my ticket to hell—
>   that's not my destination!
> Now you've got my feet on the life path,
>   all radiant from the shining of your face.
> Ever since you took my hand,
>   I'm on the right way. (Ps. 16:9–11 Message)

What a powerful picture of enjoying God's presence and pleasures—all radiant from Him! This is the life He intends for us right now, not just for someday in heaven. As A. W. Tozer said, "He meant us to see Him and live with Him and draw our life from His smile."[2] Jesus said that He came so we could have life and have it to the fullest. If we're going to know Him with that magnitude of joy, it's not going to be found wrapped up in the weight of this world. There is a clearing of rest with Him on the inside that releases His joy and pleasures, regardless of our circumstances. Our role is to become present in the presence of God.

One afternoon I was watching my two-year-old grandniece, Weslyn, race through the house with a big pacifier in her mouth. As she circled through several rooms, she periodically stopped beside someone and started to rest. Every time she paused, the same thing happened: her eyes fluttered, she began to wobble, and about the time she almost fell asleep, she suddenly caught herself and raced off again.

It was almost brutal to watch her race through the house, from person to person, blurry-eyed and weary. Why didn't she just stop, rest, and get recharged? She was so exhausted that she couldn't possibly be having fun!

Suddenly I heard that inner whisper, "Why don't *you* just stop?"

Why don't we? Why do we resist resting in Jesus? What keeps our lives stuck in fast-forward? Why don't we hit the pause button, pull back, and enjoy being present with Him? We don't have to wait until we get home from work, or until tomorrow morning when we have a quiet time, or until the weekend. Those are all important times, and they recharge us for the journey. However, you and I can go to that inner place of awareness with Him right now because *we are here . . . and so is God.*

He has given us His Spirit! We can pause, take a breath, and recalibrate our focus on Him. We can choose to adjust our spiritual posture as easily as we shift our physical posture. It's simple. We get quiet on the inside and yield to Him, becoming present with God.

Jill Briscoe tells the story of standing in line at the grocery store one day when she suddenly became aware of the presence of God. She quietly slipped off her shoes and stood there barefoot, aware she was standing on holy ground. It only takes a second to become fully present with God.

We can get quiet on the inside when we're in a meeting, taking kids to school, reading the newspaper, or having the oil changed in the car. Anywhere, anytime we can hit the pause button and be fully present with God. We can be still, turn off the noise in our heads, and know that He is God (Ps. 46:10). As we learn to live out of a place of spiritual oneness with Him and walk in step with Him every moment of the day, we can hear His whisper.

We may sense that gentle whisper of God drawing us to Himself; however, we can sometimes discount His prompting and resist slowing down to hear Him. In the West, we live in a culture that is addicted to speed. A friend told me the other day that when she gets stuck in traffic, she'll take an alternate route. She explained that it's not because another route is faster, because sometimes it isn't. "I just like to keep moving," she said.

Something in us likes to keep moving. When we're in motion, we tend to feel more productive. We live in a culture that defines value by productivity. Too often we allow the people and circumstances around us to define us instead of finding our value in belonging to God. We learn to enjoy the noise of activity and craft our lives so they are devoid of silence. Sometimes it's just easier not to hear God than to hear what He has to say, so we keep moving.

If we're honest, we may realize that we're far more driven by outside factors than we are led by the presence of God. There will always be something that competes against enjoying the awareness of God. How we respond to these things will greatly define the quality of our lives. Slowing down is a choice. What is it that keeps us in fast-forward, racing through our lives?

The Push Back

We know that we are of God, and that the whole world lies in the power of the evil one. (1 John 5:19)

There is so much that pushes back on this inner way of life. When we become more aware of the forces that try to drive us away from God, we'll be better prepared to keep our focus locked on Him. Let's take a look at three things we all struggle with that compete with living in the awareness of God's presence: the spirit of the world, Satan, and our flesh. Although these overlap, we'll look at them separately because the Bible speaks distinctly about them.

The Spirit of the World

What we have received is not the spirit of the world, but the Spirit who is from God. (1 Cor. 2:12 NIV)

The spirit of the world is in direct opposition to God. This spirit is a powerful force against our time, attention, affections, and resources. We might define the world's spirit as the collective soul of humanity that has stepped away from God. It's displayed throughout our culture. It's a sinkhole that tries to suck us away from life in His Spirit. The spirit of the world rears its head on billboards, wedges into our minds through the internet, and entices us to its way of thinking and being. The spirit of the world is everywhere, trying to push God out of the picture.

For everything in the world—the lust of the flesh, the lust of the eyes, and the pride of life—comes not from the Father but from the world. The world and its desires pass away, but whoever does the will of God lives forever. (1 John 2:16–17 NIV)

The world continually distracts us from our desire to live in communion with His presence. However, we have received the Spirit who is from God (1 Cor. 2:12). When we are yielded to God, living by His power, the world's influence loses its glitz. When we live by His Spirit from the inside, we're reminded that Christ is the only one who gives life to the fullest. It is through redirecting our attention to Him that we can hear His voice, tap into His power, and choose God over the world's way.

The Enemy

The thief comes only to steal and kill and destroy; I came that they may have life, and have it abundantly. (John 10:10)

Satan, the thief, is on a mission to try to take us out. His distractions and temptations are designed to destroy God's purpose in our lives. If Satan can keep us from being centered on God, he can pull the plug on our joy. He's out to steal our joy because it is intricately linked to our strength (Neh. 8:10). If he can cut off our joy, he can zap our strength. Either we'll become pillars of strength from God's presence or we'll be pillage for the enemy.

Do you ever wonder why it is easier to do so many other things rather than spending meaningful time with God? The enemy knows our vulnerable areas and will use them to needle away at us. Ultimately, everything in this world, including our flesh, is under the influence of the enemy's power. Even good things can be used as distractions from God. However, God is so much more powerful than the opposition. The Greater One has taken up permanent residence in us (1 Cor. 6:19). A quick choice is often all that it takes to turn us away from the enemy's ploy and to get us back on track with God's agenda.

Recently, I had one of those days where I eventually realized that I was in the vise-grip of anxiety. You know what it's like when you're caught in a mental spiral of trying to figure out a problem. You keep playing it over and over in your mind, thinking that you can bring it to a positive conclusion. The trouble is we never seem to figure out the answer. Instead, the problem grows in our minds, taking us to a place of fear in full-blown anxiety.

On that particular day, fear roared through my mind like it was a wind tunnel. I was quickly losing ground. Then this Scripture came to mind: "Submit yourselves, then, to God. Resist the devil, and he will flee from you. Come near to God and he will come near to you" (James 4:7–8 NIV). Oh my! I was trying to fight the enemy on his terms, in the natural realm of my reason. I finally brought my thoughts to God, realigning myself under His protection. I resisted the enemy in the name of Jesus and thanked God that the enemy had to leave me alone. The mental vise-grip snapped. It's not always that fast or easy. However, it is a matter of taking God at His Word and obeying Him!

God has promised that when we draw near to Him He will draw near to us. He wants us to live in that place of enjoying His presence, aware of who He is, what He has done, and what He has given us. He is God, and the enemy is no match for Him.

The Flesh

For the flesh sets its desire against the Spirit, and the Spirit against the flesh. (Gal. 5:17)

Our flesh (that is, the mind, will, emotions, and body) is constantly in opposition to the Spirit. When I first heard that truth, I wondered how I would ever overcome some things that I just seemed destined to repeat. The power of the flesh is only half the truth. Fortunately, we have help because the Spirit opposes the flesh! The Spirit is more than able to win that power struggle. This truth gives us hope. However, we have to appropriate His power.

We've all been there. It may be food, a strong desire for a person, the internet, too much time in sports, gossip, or anything that our flesh craves, but the Spirit is saying *no*. The flesh wants to feel good—even though the pleasure is temporary and may have long-term consequences. The flesh packs a powerful punch that rails against the presence of God.

There was a news story on the internet the other day that captured my curiosity. It was a video about a man riding a unicycle in a large city. But here's what got my attention: he wasn't wearing any clothes. The still photo showed much more than would normally be shown, and something in me really wanted to see the whole video. I reasoned that I was just curious—no big deal. But it was off-limits for me. It took several strong nudges of the Spirit and His help before I agreed not to make the next click. This wasn't a onetime battle; that picture kept popping up in my mind, and each time I had to *choose* not to go there.

There is hope—the Holy Spirit who dwells in us takes up the charge against our flesh. As strong as our flesh is, it's no match for God. We can yield to the flesh if we want to. However, we don't have to succumb to its demands. We can surrender to the Holy Spirit in us and rely on Him for the power to defeat our wrong desires. We make the choice, and He supplies the direction and strength.

The Spirit will make Himself known. Sometimes it's that small voice we hear on the inside. It could be a thought, a Scripture, a gentle nudge. Or the Spirit may speak to us through another person. When we sense Him we can choose to yield to Him. We can tap into His power to overcome the pounding screams of our flesh. When we say *yes* to Him, He energizes us to turn from our wrong desires and lean into His power working through us. We overcome the flesh by yielding to the Spirit and receiving His power in place of our weakness.

Yielding means surrendering our lives to God. It means coming to a place of knowing we are so safe in His love that we can say with Christ, "Not as I will, but as You will" (Matt. 26:39b). We trust Him more than feelings, reason, circumstances, or anything else. When we really know God and truly believe His radical love for us, there is perfect freedom in yielding to Him.

The Yield Sign

When you're driving your car, which is more important to you, a red light or a yield sign? The most important sign is the one right in front of you. We live with a constant "Yield to God" sign in front of us. Sometimes that sign becomes a flashing red light. It is through yielding our lives and our moments to God that His presence can lead us every step of the way. We can live in a place of purpose, power, and overcoming.

If you're having trouble recognizing God's Spirit in your life, don't get down on yourself. Stop looking at your inability and start looking at His ability! Ask God to teach you to hear His voice and He will. Go to the Bible and learn how He has spoken to people throughout the ages. Ask Him to teach you and help you grow in knowing Him. Without the anchor of Scripture, we're left to drift in our feelings and natural reason. These are fertile soil for deception. It is only in knowing what He's already said to us in the Bible that we can more clearly discern His whisper.

One of the greatest fears I once had was letting God take complete control of my life. Maybe you're like I used to be. You'd like to keep a little bit tucked away for yourself. You're glad to call on Him when you need Him, but you really want to have the option of calling your own shots. However, today I have a strong peace and great confidence in knowing that God is in control of my life.

Often we're afraid to yield our lives to God because we think He might make us do something that will cause us to be miserable. We're tempted to think that being the master of our destiny is the better route. That sounds strong, appealing, and responsible. However, it's a detour straight to destruction. We fear yielding to God because we don't know Him. If we don't know His character, it's tough to entrust our lives to Him. When self is in control, we don't want the presence of God telling us what to do. We want to go our own way.

God is the only one who knows the future and has the power to make a difference for good in the outcome of our days—now and forever. He's the only one who has the ability to take everything in our lives and miraculously work it all together for good (Rom. 8:28). This doesn't mean that we can live any way we want to and expect God to come along behind us to pick up the pieces. It means we learn to yield to His Spirit and cooperate with Him to bring about His best in every area of our lives. When we get off course or life throws us a curve, He is with us every step to bring us to His perfect place in life, in line with His greater purpose.

God can be trusted. No one else can give true purpose, restore souls, and turn messes into redemptive masterpieces. The One who loves you most is also holy, merciful, and all-powerful. He can be trusted to do more than you can ask or imagine for your life (Eph. 3:20). He is the all-good, ever-present One—all the time, every day.

Moment by Moment

Many years ago, my close friend Suzanne Best wrote a note to me about yielding to God and learning to live in the awareness of His Spirit. It has encouraged and reminded me of the simplicity of living life one moment at a time, following Him. I hope it is an encouragement to you too.

> I believe that it is possible to walk so quietly on the inside that we can hear His voice in every situation.
>
> That He can minister His peace, His secrets, His deep things to us.
>
> That we can live and move and have our being in that secret place where we walk and live by His mind and not our own, knowing that my spirit is His candle, lighting up, illuminating, giving light in every situation.
>
> That secret place where life is limitless, where wisdom and knowledge abound, direction runs freely.
>
> Oh, to be so quiet on the inside that we don't offend His gentle spirit!
>
> That we be so sensitive, that we sense His every move and desire.
>
> For we know that He will not take control, but given control, He will control.
>
> It really gets down to moment by moment, doesn't it?

God has a great life path for you that is filled with hope in Him. Experiencing the full extent of all that He offers requires living in the reality of His presence moment by moment. "In Your presence is fullness of joy; in Your right hand there are pleasures forever" (Ps. 16:11). We don't have to settle for anything less when He has given us so much more, including joy and pleasure to the fullest through His Spirit!

... Taking the **Next Step** ....

Think about It

Knowing God's presence in our daily lives is foundational to thriving in life. However, the busyness of life sometimes crowds out the intimacy of His presence. As you respond to these questions, consider how your awareness of His Spirit could shape and enrich every moment of your day.

1. If there has been a time when you were more aware of God's presence in your life, what were your impressions of that experience?
2. When difficulties come into your life, share what helps you be more aware of God's presence—circumstances, Scripture, your feelings, music, or something else? How does it influence you?
3. What would help you be more conscious of God's presence in your day-to-day activities?
4. What are some practical steps that you could take to overcome life's distractions and more fully experience God's presence?
5. In what ways might your life change if you totally relied on God's presence continually being with you?

Put It into Action

God promises that in His presence is complete joy and pleasures forever. Those are powerful benefits available to each one of us, and they are worth our focused attention. What is one step you will take this week to become more aware of God's presence in your life?

Part 2

Overcoming

You're **More** Than
Enough **in Christ**

4

Change Your Mind and Change Your Life

Renewing Your Mind with God's Word

. . . .

> Be transformed by the renewing of your mind.
>
> Romans 12:2

When I was twenty-two years old, I gave up on trying to be a Christian. I didn't tell anyone but God.

I had come to a simple faith in Christ at the age of six. It was a faith that would get me to heaven, but it didn't have legs for earth. Eventually, my young faith evolved into trying to toe the line for God by being a better rule keeper. However, it seemed like I always failed. I thought, "Maybe I'm not cut out to be a Christian." Finally, I just gave up trying.

In my midtwenties I worked with a man named Jerry. He was a Christ follower. Even though I still considered myself a Christian, his faith seemed different from mine. Jerry had a contagious energy and joy about God that spilled over into everything he did. He was a hard worker, was fun to work with, and loved everyone. Something seemed right about Jerry's relationship with God.

By the time I was twenty-eight, my life looked successful. I had a wonderful husband, a great career, a beautiful home, and vacations in Vail. But on the inside I felt empty. I didn't have peace, and I lacked real purpose. I thought about Jerry's faith and wondered if maybe there was more to Christianity than I had experienced. I was laying awake in bed one night and said a simple prayer, "God, I'm going to try to be a Christian one more time."

My husband and I went to church the next two Sundays. Instead of feeling better, I felt guilty. The second Sunday, I did what a lot of other people have done—I gave up! As I walked out the door with my husband, I thought, "I will never step foot in church again." I meant it. It was just too painful.

However, a man sitting in the choir had seen the angst and battle fatigue in my face. He raced out the side door and caught up with us. He was a distinguished looking older man with steel-white hair and was wearing a suit and tie. He gently said, "Would you like to go back inside and pray?"

I wanted to go in, but I waited to see if my husband would go. Thankfully, he agreed and we both went in and knelt down at the altar. That day I came home to Jesus. I gave my past, present, and future—all my life—to Jesus. I asked Him to forgive me for all the things I had done wrong. In exchange He gave me forgiveness, peace, and purpose. Later my husband told me that he had prayed a similar prayer.

That afternoon I was playing tennis when the tornado sirens went off. We lived in a tornado alley, so we always took warnings very seriously. I stopped to listen, but instead of feeling fear, I felt an enormous joy come over me. I remember dropping my racket to my side and standing there grinning because I knew I was forgiven and would go to heaven if I died.

God knows how to capture our weary hearts.

First Things First

I spent a lot of frustrated years trying to figure out spiritual matters in my life. I want to share with you what I wish I had known many years earlier about knowing God. This isn't intended to answer all your questions; it is simply information that could have helped me. I hope it will help you too. It's a brief summary of how we can come to God through Christ to be forgiven of all of our sin and have eternal life. This is the first step to experiencing all that God offers us. Before reading it, and if you want to, ask God to help you know Him better.

When we read the Bible, we aren't just reading words that came from the minds of men in millenniums past, because "all Scripture is inspired by God" (2 Tim. 3:16). He breathed His life into the words that were penned. The Bible is the only book that has been validated by multiple fulfilled prophecies, authenticating God's inspiration of its writings. This unique fact sets it apart from all other books. It has been said that there is enough evidence to validate the Bible's authenticity but not so much as to negate the need for faith to believe it. If we want to know about God we can go to the primary source—the Bible.

Some people wonder why we need Jesus to have a relationship with God. He came to bridge the gap between us and God. While God is love, He is also holy and just. His justice has said, "the wages of sin is death" (Rom. 6:23). We need help with making that payment because we have all sinned (Rom. 3:23). Fortunately, He tells us where to find help: "but the free gift of God is eternal life in Christ Jesus our Lord" (Rom. 6:23).

The payment plan is in the person of Jesus, who offers forgiveness and eternal life. Have you ever wondered why the cross and the resurrection are so significant? It goes back to death being the payment for our sin. Jesus came to earth as all God and all man. He never once sinned. He was perfectly holy and He fulfilled Old Testament prophecies about the

Messiah. He was divine, born of a virgin. His divinity set Him apart from all others. As all God and all man, He had the power to take our sin upon Himself, die in our place, pay the price we owed—in full—and then be resurrected back to life to be our Savior and Lord. His death as our substitute satisfied the demands of God's justice and holiness. And now He offers us His salvation as a free gift—the greatest expression of love that has ever been extended.

Does that mean that everyone is automatically forgiven and has eternal life? No. It means the gift is *available* to everyone who trusts in Jesus, in who He is and what He did for us. The gift is located "in Christ Jesus our Lord." We accept the gift and the Giver of eternal life by yielding our lives to Christ and trusting that He died and rose for us. As the Bible says:

> If you confess with your mouth Jesus as Lord, and believe in your heart that God raised Him from the dead, you will be saved; for with the heart a person believes, resulting in righteousness, and with the mouth he confesses, resulting in salvation. (Rom. 10:9–10)

When we trust Christ we turn toward Him instead of going our own way. We do that by praying something along these lines, realizing it's our heart that He is listening to:

Jesus, I am turning from my own way to follow you. I believe You are God's Son and that You substituted Your life for mine when You died on the cross and rose from the dead. I trust that You paid for all of my sin. Jesus, will You forgive me and take charge of my life? I receive You as my Lord and Savior. Thank You for forgiving me and giving me eternal life!

If you haven't yielded to Jesus in faith but want to, then why not talk to Him and tell Him so right now? Just tell Him—from your heart—the thoughts in that last paragraph. He loves you and will always say yes to this kind of sincere prayer. When we come to Christ in faith He gives us eternal life and makes us spiritually brand-new.

It's that simple. When we experience spiritual rebirth through Christ we begin a brand-new relationship with God. Maybe you already personally know Christ but you haven't been following Him. Why not turn back to Him right now? He loves you.

As with any relationship, we need to grow in knowing God. That step begins by renewing our mind through His Word.

Renewing the Mind

A few years ago I bought my current condo. It was in a good location and had good bones, but it needed updates. As soon as I moved in, I went to work. A friend who owned a painting business generously sent a team to paint it. I updated the kitchen and a few other things. I could have lived in it the way it was, but I wanted my home to reflect me—not the previous owners.

In a similar way, ownership immediately changes when we come to faith in Christ. Our spirit is made brand-new with His Spirit. We get a fresh start in life with all of our sins forgiven. The Bible puts it this way:

> Therefore, if anyone is in Christ, the new creation has come. The old has gone, the new is here! (2 Cor. 5:17 NIV)

While our spirit is immediately made new, we still have the same mind. Our minds have to be renewed. All the old wrong ways of thinking and acting have to be upgraded to become more like Christ.

> And do not be conformed to this world, but be transformed by the renewing of your mind, so that you may prove what the will of God is, that which is good and acceptable and perfect. (Rom. 12:2)

Nancy, the wife of my former co-worker Jerry, taught me how the Bible is our resource to renew our minds. It makes a practical difference in our lives. Whether we need wisdom, direction, courage, strength, or encouragement, it's all there. God's Word offers us more than we can imagine.

About two weeks after Nancy began helping me along in my journey, I got concerned that I would fall back to my old ways. I had made so many recommitments to Christ over the years and had repeatedly failed. I told her, "I'm afraid that this commitment won't stick either." She threw back her head, laughed, and said, "Oh Nancy, don't you know that you are saved by grace and you are kept by grace?"

No, I didn't know that truth. Suddenly, there was hope for me that didn't depend on me!

The Bible tells us, "By grace you have been saved through faith; and that not of yourselves, it is the gift of God" (Eph. 2:8). It also teaches us, "Therefore as you have received Christ Jesus the Lord, so walk in Him, having been firmly rooted and now being built up in Him and established in your faith" (Col. 2:6–7). We don't shift from grace and faith into trying harder. Knowing these truths puts a spring in our step on our spiritual journey.

Maybe you're thinking you need someone to teach you. I was very fortunate in having Nancy's guidance. However, if you want to know God better, just ask Him to teach you. He likes to answer that prayer! Get into the Bible and start reading in the New Testament—it's all about Jesus. Find a solid Christian church that teaches the Bible and take a class. Ask God to connect you with people who know and love His Word. The same God who meets me will meet you because He loves you and wants to help you to continually renew your mind.

Enjoy Reading the Bible

While I was teaching at a Christian college, Dr. Charles Miller from California came and spoke at one of our department meetings. We were all eager to hear Miller and were seated around a conference table. I had never heard him, so I didn't know what to expect. He told us to get out a pen and paper and turn in our Bibles to a passage in Isaiah. (You probably remember that "Get out a pen and paper" is code for "Pop quiz!")

I glanced around the table at the professors with their doctorates, and I felt enormously inadequate. The palms of my hands started to sweat. I was afraid I might have to share my insights alongside these scholars.

Miller continued, "Now, I want you to read this passage and *enjoy it*. That's all I want you to do is just *enjoy* these Scriptures. If something seems to pop out at you, jot it down. If not, that's fine too."

I was disarmed by simplicity: enjoy reading the Bible. That's it. We weren't to dissect it, outline it, research the original languages, identify three major points, draw out applications, or fill in any blanks. *Enjoy* the Scriptures and see if anything pops out—really?

As we read the Scriptures, each of us uniquely encountered God in His Word. We all heard God speaking to us through the Bible. That experience marked the way I have read, studied, and taught the Bible ever since.

When we seek God through reading the Bible, He ignites His Word to us and reveals Himself. Knowing Him better changes us. Maybe you've tried reading the Bible and nothing special happened to you. Maybe it felt boring or pointless, and you wondered what you were missing. Talk to Him about that and ask Him to help you know Him better.

Learn a Better Navigation System

This past fall, my sister Carole and I were on vacation and driving to the lake. I knew the area better because I had been there many times. This was her first visit. However, she had the map. Since I was driving, I used my directions. We came to a crossroads, and Carole said we needed to turn. I graciously resisted. We pulled over and shared a few sisterly words. She was relentless. As she showed me the map, I silently grumbled about her stubbornness.

That is, I grumbled until I realized she was right. (It is still easier to say, "She was right" instead of, "I was wrong"!) Something in me wanted to keep going my way. However, if I didn't follow her instructions, we would have made fast time to the wrong destination.

When we realize that correction from God's Word is profitable to us, it will change the way we read the Bible. When He shows us that we are going the wrong way, it is to protect us. We never have to fear ending up in the wrong place if we follow God's Word. It may not be easy to change directions; however, it will ultimately always be good.

Change is seldom easy. Recently I began a new fitness class. I didn't go because I liked working out; I went because I needed the benefit of the training. We know that the right kind of exercise profits our bodies—if we do it! The Word of God is the same way. It has to be taken into our lives and exercised if it is going to benefit us. Then it becomes "profitable for teaching, for reproof, for correction, for training in righteousness" (2 Tim. 3:16). Those benefits will positively affect every area of our lives.

The first year that I began studying the Bible, I wanted to learn everything I could as soon as I could. I was a little overly ambitious. Other, more mature Christians had worn, marked-up Bibles. I wanted mine to look like theirs. My Bible was my new status symbol. I wanted to be part of the "in" crowd. I underlined and highlighted with fervency. I remember getting in the car after church one day and tossing it in the backseat. I did whatever I could to speed up the wear and tear.

However, it takes time to grow in our relationship with God. He loves us and He is patient with us. Knowing His Word takes time. It's not about carrying worn-out Bibles and spouting off verses. It *is* about becoming more like Jesus.

Last night, one of my friends told me that she has been praying, "God, change me from the inside out." She realized she had a critical attitude toward someone. My friend wants her life to line up with Jesus. God began showing her that her attitude came from wanting to change some of the habits of the other person. When she let go of her desire to change that person, God changed my friend on the inside and the critical attitude left.

Knowing the Bible gives us practical help in our attitudes, relationships, and everyday decisions. Years ago, I was in the process of making a change in my retirement funds. On someone's recommendation I quickly made some stock moves. There's nothing wrong with that, as it's often exactly what is needed. However, before I sold the stock, a verse popped into my mind: "He who makes haste to be rich will not go unpunished" (Prov. 28:20).

In that particular situation, I sensed that the verse was telling me to slow down and hit the pause button. I rationalized, disregarded its counsel, and ended up losing money. God's Word will give us wisdom for our everyday lives. Of course, just because a Scripture pops into our mind does not always mean it is God speaking in the circumstance. After all, Satan used Scripture to tempt Jesus. However, we can learn to hear God's wisdom through the Bible to make correct applications.

We can grow in knowing and trusting God. One of the main ways this happens is through reading the Bible in its proper context, praying for understanding, and learning to apply it in our lives. We can believe that everything God says is to help us in our journey to be more like Christ. He will give purpose to your life, enable you to be who He created you to be, and empower you to live to the fullest.

If you're like me, some days you just get weary of acting like yourself and you want to be more like Jesus. Be patient. We will be growing spiritually for the rest of our lives. Ruth Graham's epitaph says it best: "End of Construction: Thank You for Your Patience."

One-on-One with God

Recently, I was out in the early morning light photographing the historic Cana lighthouse on the Wisconsin shore of Lake Michigan. As is often the case, the water was low enough to walk across a rock embankment to reach the tiny island. It was a crisp fall day, blue-green waves were lapping the shore, and the scene was magnificent. I positioned myself on the craggy rocks of the extended shoreline, faced the lighthouse, and set up my camera on the tripod.

Just as I was framing the perfect shot, one side of my tripod began sinking. "But I'm on a solid rock!" I thought. I realized that I had left one tripod leg loose and everything was falling apart. Tightening the legs on a camera tripod is basic knowledge. Those legs are the camera's foundation. If you don't have stability, you will have problems and maybe even lose your camera in a lake. In photography, as with so many things in life, if you don't take care of the basics, you will be robbed of the beauty that could be yours.

In our spiritual lives, it is sometimes easy to become too casual with the basics. We know we need time with God in His Word, we need interaction with Him, and we need to put into action what He is teaching us. The Word, prayer, and application are the tripod of our personal fellowship with God. However, sometimes we put aside the basics and wonder why we're struggling. Our individual time with God overflows into our relationships, work, church, finances, community, service, and every area of our lives.

There is no substitute for personal time alone with God in His Word. That is the main way that our faith will grow, because faith comes by hearing God's Word (Rom. 10:17). Corporate worship, community, equipping, serving, and giving are integral to our spiritual development and vitality. As important as these things are, however, they aren't a substitute for our one-on-one time with God. It is foundational that we spend time in the awareness of His presence, listening to

Him, worshiping Him, experiencing Him in the Scriptures so that He can transform our lives. As we go out to live the life He calls us to, our transformation continues throughout the day as we walk with Him.

The change that God brings through spending time with Him gradually transforms us into being more and more like Jesus. "But we all, with unveiled face, beholding as in a mirror the glory of the Lord, are being transformed into the same image from glory to glory, just as from the Lord, the Spirit" (2 Cor. 3:18). The mirror is the Word of God. As we spend time seeing Jesus in the Bible, He gradually changes us by His Spirit into the image that we are seeing.

Have you ever been around someone for so long that you start using the same phrases? One of my closest friends from college commented a few years ago that some of our mannerisms and expressions are similar. Even though we live in different states, we've spent enough time together over the years that we've rubbed off on each other in good ways. That's how it is with God. Everything from Him that rubs off on us is positive. We'll never pick up a bad habit, wrong words, put-downs, or negative attitudes from Him. He always loves us into being more and more like Jesus.

The process of renewing our minds to be like Him takes place so gradually that we usually don't realize it's happening. I was stunned one night when I slammed my little toe into the bed and the word "mmmmph" came out of my mouth. Somewhere along the way, old words had been replaced with "mmmmph." It's amazing how God renews our minds when we take time to meet Him in his Word.

Reading the Bible Relationally

As I begin reading the Bible each morning, I usually start by saying something like this simple prayer: "Lord, will you help me know You better and love You more?" I come to His

Word expecting to hear from Him. Then I read the Bible relationally, meaning that I interact with Him through talking and listening as I read. I ask Him what He means and how that truth applies to my life. I ask Him to help me be and do what I see in the Bible.

This morning my devotional reading included part of Jesus's Sermon on the Mount from Matthew 5. I sort of groaned inside. I seldom enjoy reading that passage, so I started to skip that section. (Just being honest!) However, instead of finding something more to my liking, I said, "Lord, I dread reading those verses because I fall so short of the standard they set." He already knew what I was thinking. I sensed His reply, "Read them anyway!" I did and He nudged me a little closer toward being more like Jesus.

Sometimes it's a challenge to settle down and spend time with God. We don't always feel like having this one-on-one time. I've found the best time for me to spend with God in His Word and prayer is early every morning, along with a strong cup of coffee. If I start doing something else, such as reading and answering emails, I quickly become distracted, move on to the next task, and the day gets away from me.

Author Stuart Briscoe is fond of saying, "Don't let your head hit the pillow until your nose has been in the Book." Briscoe understands the value of investing time in the Bible. He's lived his life that way. Now in his eighties, he's still got his nose in the Book!

From a cost-to-benefit standpoint, the wisdom and direction that God's Word gives us far exceeds our time investment. It pays dividends in every area of our lives. However, we don't read and study it just to gain more knowledge, because that motivation can bring pride. God expects us to apply what He is teaching us, and that requires humility.

If we dismiss the relational component in reading the Bible, our devotional and study time can shrivel up into a lifeless activity of dead knowledge. It can become just one more thing on our to-do list. The more relational we are in our study, the more we'll enjoy spending time with the Lord.

If you're not enjoying a daily devotional time with God, here are a few practical things that can help you. You will find that the more time you spend with Him the more you will enjoy being with Him.

Holy Spirit. Ask God to meet with you through His Word. "Would you help me to know You better and love You more?" Expect to hear the whisper of His Spirit.

Bible. Have a good modern translation of the Bible that you understand.[1] It's a bonus if you can have one that has some study helps in it.

Read relationally. As you're reading, remember to *read relationally* by talking with God and listening for Him. Stop and interact with Him as you read.

Pen and paper. Keep a pen and notepad handy. Jot down anything that seems to "pop out" to you and talk to Him about it.

Place. Find a place where you can have some undistracted time alone. For some of you, this may not physically be possible. That's okay. You can still meet with God. Ask Him to help you stay focused.

Time. Find the time that works best to be one-on-one with God. If you can't find the time, then time probably isn't the problem—it's prioritizing your time.

Later list. If you're like me, as soon as you sit down with God, you may get distracted by things that need to be done. Keep a "later list" and jot those things down to do later.

Prayer and application. Spend time talking with God specifically about how you can apply what He is teaching you. Then practice what you read. Talk to Him about the things on your mind and heart. Then throughout the day, keep your conversation with God ongoing!

That's all you need to have a devotional time with God. Keep the main thing the main thing. Beyond the basics, here are other possible helps.

Reading schedule. A good Bible reading schedule can help you read through the Bible a few chapters a day. But *stay flexible*—it's a guide, not a rule. It's not about quantity; it's about engaging with God. A schedule gives specific passages to read each day. Otherwise, we tend to focus on only a few parts of the Bible. I've used Robert Murray McCheyne's schedule for almost two decades. Thanks to a graduate professor recommending it to me, it helped change my devotional time. The reading plan is available at various online sites.[2] You may want to divide up your reading time between morning and night. If you don't have a guide, read one chapter from the Old and New Testaments each day, and one from Psalms or Proverbs.

Journal. If you like to reflect and write in a journal, then enjoy this process. If that's not for you, you're no less spiritual. Do what helps you engage with God in His Word.

Psalm 119. This passage can whet your appetite for God's Word. It's one of the sections I go to when I need a fresh jump start to enjoying the Bible.

Make it sustainable. Start where you are with the amount of time you have today. You can always expand your time.

Supplemental materials. Worship music, teaching messages, study tools,[3] and books can be helpful. However, remember these things are a supplement—*not* a substitution—for being in the Bible with God.

Find out what fits you and keep doing it. It's okay to start with five or six minutes. Many years ago, I purposed to read the Bible at least five minutes every day. While I usually read more than five minutes, that one decision has served me well over the years, especially on days when I might not have read anything. It's better to start with a few minutes and build from that than to be overly ambitious, become frustrated, and quit. There will be times when you can do more. If so, do it. The goal is to establish consistency every day. The point isn't to have a devotional time. The point is to meet with God, know Him better, love Him more—and enjoy being with Him! As you do, He will change you.

Knowing God More Intimately

There is a passage of Scripture that can help change the way you and I come to God and read the Bible. Brand it in your heart. It's a prayer that gives us insight into His desire for us to know Him and all that He offers us. We can pray it throughout our lives.

> I keep asking that the God of our Lord Jesus Christ, the glorious Father, may give you the Spirit of wisdom and revelation, so that you may know him better. I pray that the eyes of your heart may be enlightened in order that you may know the hope to which he has called you, the riches of his glorious inheritance in his holy people, and his incomparably great power for us who believe. (Eph. 1:17–19 NIV)

This is a passage that we can pray in the first person for ourselves, "I pray that the eyes of *my* understanding may be enlightened . . ." I pray this passage for myself and for other people. I have experienced God opening my eyes to see new insights. He has continually helped me know Him better. This is a prayer that God loves to answer because it's His will for us.

Reading the Bible and renewing our minds is about knowing God better and loving Him more. It's about bringing our lives into and under the power of His life. As we do, we get a clearer view of Him, and He changes us from the inside out to become more like Jesus. A. W. Tozer said it so well:

> The Bible is not an end in itself, but a means to bring men [and women] to an intimate and satisfying knowledge of God, that they may enter into Him, that they may delight in His presence, may taste and know the inner sweetness of the very God Himself in the core and center of their hearts.[4]

Lord, make it so in our lives!

. . . Taking the **Next Step** . . . .

God's Word can change our lives for the better. We can either become more like the world or, through the Bible, become more like Jesus. The choice is ours. Renewing our minds will be ongoing for the rest of our lives. To be more like Jesus, we will need to spend time with Him in His Word. It is our avenue to enjoying and loving Him more.

Think about It

1. What are some practical areas of your life where you would like the benefit of God changing you?
2. In what ways might the Bible help you grow or overcome in those areas?
3. What might enhance your enjoyment of your devotional time?
4. In what ways could reading the Bible relationally make God's Word more intimate for you?
5. If you had to choose one, which of these do you sense you need to grow in: (1) spending time in the Bible,

(2) talking with God, (3) applying what you're learning, or (4) enjoying God more in your private devotions? Ask God to help you in that area.

Put It into Action

What is one practical thing you will do this week to help you renew your mind with God's Word?

You're Better Than That!

Knowing Who You Are in Christ

· · · · · · · · · · · · · · · · · · ·

Christ in you, the hope of glory.
Colossians 1:27

When my marriage hit the wall, hope felt in short supply. I knew that God was in control; however, I felt like my life had run off the tracks. I was praying, spending time with God in His Word, and doing everything I knew to do. Even with self-help books, friends, and my small group at church, it felt like life was unraveling. My self-confidence shriveled.

Maybe you've experienced that "less than" feeling too. But all the while something in us is screaming, "I'm better than that!" I did something that I never thought I would do. I went to counseling. I found an excellent Christian counselor and began with these words: "If my marriage stays together, I'm going to need a lot of help. If my marriage fails, I'm going to need a lot of help. Either way, I need help!"

The day came when the counselor told me that I had completed individual sessions and needed to go to small group sessions. My first thought was, "Not me!" I wasn't about to bare my soul to a bunch of strangers. Besides, I was going through a divorce—I wasn't going crazy!

It took a huge dose of humility to walk into group that first night, but I was desperate. As I listened to the women's stories, I learned that most of them had suffered from serious abuse. I knew that *they* needed help.

The second time that we met, my pain was much greater than my pride. If emotions could bleed, I would have been swimming in my blood. When I opened up to share, the pride broke and all the hurt, anger, and disappointment spilled out. I cried like I'd never cried before. I didn't care what anybody thought.

What happened next stunned me. After I had exposed my pain and tears to the group, the women spontaneously got up, surrounded me, hugged me, and started praying over me and asking for God's healing. It was probably the most powerful encounter with God and the body of Christ that I have ever experienced. In the messiest, weakest, did-not-have-it-together time of my life, I was loved.

For many of us, brokenness is the superhighway that God uses to help drive pride out of our lives. However, God never leaves His wounded on the side of the road. Pride is a false image. He wants it replaced with humility, which allows us to fully receive *His* image.

During that difficult season of life, the truth of who I am in Christ began to take hold. If you had asked me before, I could have given you the theological answers for my identity in Christ. However, when more of me got emptied out, there was room for more of Him. I came to more fully understand who I am and what I have in Christ. Gradually, He began leading me into my true identity in Him.

God loves us so much that He gives us a new identity—His very own—through Jesus. Our broken image is renewed and new hope is infused into our lives as we learn who we are in Christ.

The Truth That Brings Freedom

Recently in the media there was the story of an inmate who, after serving twenty-two years in prison, was found innocent by new DNA evidence. Did the truth of the DNA set him free? The truth was there all those years he sat in prison, but it didn't set him free. It was the *knowledge* brought by the DNA testing—*that* truth set him free.

We often hear people say, "The truth will set you free." That sounds good, but it's only part of the truth that Jesus spoke. His actual words were, "If you continue in My word, then you are truly disciples of Mine; and you will know the truth, and the truth will make you free" (John 8:31–32). *Continue* means that we come to know, understand, and apply His words in our everyday lives.

In our relationship with Christ, He promises that three things happen as His Word becomes an integral part of our lives:

1. We are truly His followers.
2. We will know the truth.
3. That known truth will set us free.

Knowing and living in God's Word will teach us how to experience all that He has given us in Christ.

God's truth is written in the Bible. Just as the truth of the DNA testing had to be known for the prisoner to go free, we have to know God's truth to experience its power in our lives.

A short time after my faith renewal in my late twenties, Nancy, the friend who was helping me learn more about God, casually mentioned, "You don't have to sin if you don't want to." A bit stunned, I said, "What are you talking about?" That was a brand-new concept for me.

Sometimes it seems the pull of temptation is so powerful and there is no other choice but to sin. Good news alert: that's not true!

> For sin shall no longer be your master, because you are not under the law, but under grace. (Rom. 6:14 NIV)

We have been snatched from behind enemy lines and brought into God's kingdom (Col. 1:13). If we are in Christ, nothing is powerful enough to force us to be slaves to sin. In fact, the Bible promises that there will always be a way out when we face every temptation.

> No temptation has overtaken you except what is common to mankind. And God is faithful; he will not let you be tempted beyond what you can bear. But when you are tempted, he will also provide a way out so that you can endure it. (1 Cor. 10:13 NIV)

That truth gives us legs and enables us to run from temptation. All we have to do is look for the escape route and take it. Knowing this truth can save us from repeated failures. God has a better life for us!

You Are Righteous

How often have you heard Christians say, "I'm just a sinner saved by grace"? It might sound humble if we don't know any better. However, it's another half-truth that can drag us down. We need whole truths to thrive in life. Here's the rest of that truth: you and I were sinners, we have been saved, and now we are righteous in Christ.

This truth is intricately connected to our understanding that the power of sin has been broken in our lives. Jesus paid for our sins and made a way for us to have eternal life. The justice of God was fulfilled in Christ, and now we have a right relationship with Him. In Christ He places His righteous character—His holiness and innocence—in us. It is a gift from God in our spiritual rebirth, not something that we can reach on our own.

> God made him who had no sin to be sin for us, so that in him we might become the righteousness of God. (2 Cor. 5:21 NIV)

We receive His righteousness by faith, not by trying to be better. Have you ever felt more right with God because you went to church, had a really special devotional time, or did something good? I have. I've even had times when I felt like I was on a spiritual roll and thought, "I need to ask God for something really big right now because I think He's listening!"

While praying and going to church are good things, they don't give us a better standing with God. Only Jesus gives us rightness with God, and He has given us *His* righteousness. Right actions can and will come out of righteousness. However, they do not create our righteousness; that only comes through Christ's work on our behalf.

> Not having a righteousness of my own derived from the Law, but that which is through faith in Christ, the righteousness which comes from God on the basis of faith. (Phil. 3:9)

In addition to giving us a right relationship with God, what practical application does Christ's righteousness have in our lives? Do we look spiritual, spout Scripture, and act religious? An example of righteousness at work could be seen in trying to forgive someone who has deeply hurt us. Our natural tendency would be to say that the offense is too big; that person doesn't deserve to be forgiven and we cannot forgive him or her. However, we can realize that Christ's righteousness is in us helping us to *do the right thing*. When I forgave my former husband, it wasn't because I felt like forgiving him. I needed to forgive him because it was the right thing to do—and through Christ I had the ability and the power to do the right thing.

God's grace is at work empowering us to become like Christ. We can confidently say, "God, I can't forgive that person in my own strength. However, I am in Christ, and I can do all things through Him. You have given me Your righteousness. I choose to forgive." Having the proper inner image empowers us to live rightly before God and people. That image develops as we *know* the truth in His Word.

You Are a Saint

When we think of saints we usually think of someone like Saint Francis or Mother Teresa, people who we consider truly great Christians. I'm currently reading a novel about Saint Francis of Assisi. He was an extraordinary man whose life was radically abandoned to Christ. Although he lived almost eight hundred years ago, his life is still studied as a model for Christianity.

When we hear someone say, "Well, I'm no saint," we usually understand them to mean that they aren't perfect. However, Jesus's followers are addressed as saints in the New Testament. That means Christ lives on the inside of each of us and has set us apart. It's His holiness in us. Our bodies become temples of His Holy Spirit (1 Cor. 6:19). If our inner image as righteous saints is stronger than our image as sinners, it will help change the way we live our lives. This comes by knowing and growing in our new identity in Christ.

We've all seen a pro football player get traded to a new team. At the very first news conference, he'll have on the new team's cap or jersey. He's talking about how glad he is to be on the new team. From the moment he's traded, everything in his life starts changing to help him identify with his new team. In order to succeed, he has to let go of his old team's identity and take on his new team's identity.

In a similar way, when we are in Christ, we need to put off our former identity and learn to "put on the new self, which in the likeness of God has been created in righteousness and holiness of the truth" (Eph. 4:24). As we do, His freedom, power, and likeness become more real in our lives. We can love with His love. We can forgive with His forgiveness. We can live in ways that will honor Christ and bear much fruit.

You Are Forgiven

Recently, I was teaching in a women's prison. During our Q&A time, a beautiful young woman broke down and wept with guilt, shame, and regret. She said that she knew God had forgiven her; however, she couldn't forgive herself for what she had done. Then she asked a question that torments many people: "How can I ever forgive myself?"

We don't have to live in a prison to be imprisoned by our past. When we come face-to-face with our sin it can feel overwhelming. If our sin ever looks too big to be forgiven, we need a greater understanding of God's mercy toward us. If the substitution of Jesus on the cross for our sins is enough to satisfy God's holy demand for justice—and it is—then it is also enough for you and me. We can forgive ourselves through receiving Christ's payment for our sin.

> In him we have redemption through his blood, the forgiveness of sins. (Eph. 1:7 NIV)

There is no sin that you or I can commit that is greater than the power of Jesus's blood to forgive it. When Jesus walked on earth He was divine—all God and also all man. Because of Christ's divinity, His death, resurrection, and blood had the power to pay the penalty for sin. He was and is our substitute. God accepted Jesus's sacrifice for *all* of our sin.

Not only does God offer forgiveness for our sins, He also cleanses our conscience from those sins.

> How much more, then, will the blood of Christ, who through the eternal Spirit offered himself unblemished to God, cleanse our consciences from acts that lead to death, so that we may serve the living God! (Heb. 9:14 NIV)

Through Christ we are spiritually scrubbed clean! Our role is to receive Jesus *and* receive what He has done. He is the one "who loves us and has freed us from our sins by his blood" (Rev. 1:5 NIV).

At the age of nineteen, author and friend Linda Strom found herself in the middle of a divorce with no job and no means of financial support. She also had a two-year-old son, Terry, who meant the world to her. The decision was made to leave her son with his grandparents while she trained for a job in another state. It was the most painful time of her life and a decision that could never be changed.

After a year, she was reunited with her child, but the regret of her circumstances and choices lingered for years. Linda became a Christ follower and received forgiveness. She also repeatedly asked her son for forgiveness. When he started using drugs as a teenager, she took full responsibility for his choices. She lived with regret and shame, and he used the regret to his advantage. She was not free, and neither was he.

One night while Linda was on her knees, the experience of God's forgiveness and cleansing moved from her head to her heart. She truly knew she was completely forgiven. She stopped living in the land of regret. The next time her son tried to tap into her past mistakes and pain, her response was, "The regrets account is closed. Empty . . . insufficient funds." That day she told her son the truth that God had forgiven her.

Another wonderful part of this story is that Terry found accountability and freedom by dealing with his own issues through counseling and a twelve-step program. He is now teaching recovery, and he and his mother tell their story to others.

When God's forgiveness truly moves from our head down to our heart, forgiveness for ourselves flows with it.

Agree with God—"I'm Better Than That"

One of the best mystery books I have ever read is the classic *Gaudy Night* by Dorothy Sayers. The lead character in the story, Harriet Vane, returns to Oxford for her class reunion. While there, she learns that someone is tormenting the faculty and issuing death threats. Finally, after some nail-biting encounters, the evildoer is caught and confesses to the dirty deeds.

When we think of confession, we usually think of a person getting caught and admitting that they have done something wrong. We understand the concept and know to confess our sins. However, making a confession means we agree with something, whether good or bad. There is a positive side of confession that we can apply in our lives. It's agreeing with God's Word about what He has done for us and given to us.

An example of this type of confession would be declaring what God says about us instead of what we feel about ourselves. We could say, "I feel so worthless," or we could agree with what God says, that "I am fearfully and wonderfully made" (Ps. 139:14). One statement focuses on feelings, the other statement agrees with God's Word. We could say, "I'm just a sinner" or we could agree with God and say, "I am forgiven and I am the righteousness of God in Christ Jesus." The latter will help us to develop a mindset in line with God's Word.

If we are going to enjoy the full benefit of Christ's abundant life, our motives, actions, and words will need to line up with His Word. Most of us understand the importance of our motives and actions. However, the Bible also emphasizes the importance of our words. Jesus said, "For the mouth speaks out of that which fills the heart" (Matt. 12:34). If we realize we are saying things that don't agree with what God says, we need to stop and remember, "In Christ, I'm better than that!" We can choose to put good words that agree with His truth into our hearts, knowing that words carry power.

"Death and life are in the power of the tongue, and those who love it will eat its fruit" (Prov. 18:21). This verse gives all new meaning to the phrase "I had to eat my words." Do you want your words to produce life or death? You get to decide. Years ago in the margin of my Bible I wrote, "I will use my tongue to speak words of life." I've purposed to live in that truth, even though I've sometimes fallen short.

How does this apply? Maybe you're having a particularly difficult day. You may feel like nothing is going your way. Those are the times when you're tempted to say, "This is an awful day. Nothing ever goes right for me!" Who did those words just agree with—the enemy or God?

Maybe you're thinking, "Well, that's how I feel some days, and I'm not going to lie about it." But there is a greater truth available to you than your feelings—God's Word. His words are more important and powerful than how you feel. His words can produce life even when you feel at your worst—because *He is life.* You could say, "God, today's a challenging day, but I'm not going to let it get me down. The Greater One lives in me! Thank You that You're working all things together for good because I love You and follow You. Thank You that no weapon formed against me will prosper."

Which words would you rather eat? One set of words is negative and will work against you—they cooperate with the enemy. As one of my friends said this week, "I do not want to be doing the work of the enemy!" The other words will bring you up to a higher level than your emotions; they cooperate with God's will. Speak words that agree with God, words that will stir your faith and unleash His purpose in your life.

No More Condemnation

Do you ever sense a cloud of guilt hanging over your head, even though you haven't done anything specifically wrong? Maybe it's a vague feeling that you haven't done enough or don't quite measure up. Condemnation can make you feel that way. It's that feeling of being under a sentence of guilt and judgment. Conviction is the Holy Spirit telling you to repent of a wrongdoing. Condemnation is a false accusation against you that doesn't come from God. Condemnation presses you down. Conviction calls you up higher to Him.

When a police car pulled out behind me the other day, I wasn't guilty, but I felt guilty. My feelings were carried over from long past experiences with police cars behind me. That's how condemnation hooks us; it draws us back to our past. It attacks our innocence that we have been given in Christ. It can masquerade as a feeling that we always need to do more, that we're a failure, or that nothing we do is quite good enough. It's one of the enemy's big guns. He pulls it out to try and remind us that we don't deserve the mercy and grace God has given us. We don't deserve it, but we don't have to. If we deserved it, then it wouldn't be mercy and grace! For those of us in Christ, God never condemns us.

> Therefore, there is now no condemnation for those who are in Christ Jesus, because through Christ Jesus the law of the Spirit who gives life has set you free from the law of sin and death. (Rom. 8:1–2 NIV)

In Christ we are free from the sentence of death for our sins. There is no condemnation for us. The superior law of the Spirit of life in Christ has freed us from the law of sin and death. The Greater One lives in us and the penalty of sin is no longer on us.

Condemnation reminds me of my first debt. When I was in high school, I bought several 8-track tapes (ancient music recordings). I opened my first credit account through a local business and charged the full cost of $15. I worried about how I was ever going to pay off a debt that size. It felt huge! When I made the last payment, it was like iron chains had been lifted off of me.

It would be foolish today if I kept trying to pay off those 8-track tapes. The law of payment is greater than the law of debt because payment fulfills debt. However, many Christians are still living under the weight of something that Jesus paid off over two thousand years ago.

Condemnation is the enemy's sucker punch to try to knock us down and keep us down. Don't fall for it. Your life is now operating under a superior law, the law of life in Christ Jesus! "If the Son sets you free, you will be free indeed" (John 8:36 NIV).

When the accusation of condemnation pops into your mind or emotions, meet it head-on with the truth. Confess Romans 8:1 to God and thank Him: "There is now no condemnation for those who are in Christ Jesus." Agree with Him that in Christ you are free from all condemnation. That's the verse I run to when I feel the enemy is accusing me. I agree with God's Word and get under His protection. When I do this, it also gets my mind off of me and onto Jesus, enabling me to resist condemnation. It works every time! This is how I speak that truth:

> *Father, thank You that there is now no condemnation in me, because I am in Christ Jesus. Thank You that Jesus has paid the debt for my sin. My account with You is paid in full. Thank You that I am free of all condemnation. Thank You that Your superior law of life in Christ Jesus has set me free from the lower law of sin and death.*

Speak Words of Blessing

If you are a follower of Christ, you are blessed regardless of your circumstances.

Blessed be the God and Father of our Lord Jesus Christ, who has blessed us with every spiritual blessing in the heavenly places in Christ. (Eph. 1:3)

When I learned that "blessed of God" really means to "cause to prosper," it set an entirely different perspective on understanding God's desire to bless us. Imagine the power of that truth as God says over and over in the Bible that He causes us to prosper. What is this prosperity that He is referring to? It is everything good that He has promised and purposed for our lives. It is all the good that He wants to happen in and through our lives to fulfill His greater plan.

If we were to do a study on the blessings of God, we would see that they started from the very beginning when He blessed Adam and Eve in the Garden of Eden. The blessing continued through Abraham, right through Jesus, and straight into our lives.

It is especially important to agree with God when we don't *feel* blessed. The blessings that God has given us in the heavenly realm have authority over the natural realm. The enemy will try to wear us down by our feelings, thoughts, and circumstances. However, we can stand on God's Word, confident His truth will ultimately prevail. If He says that we are blessed—and He does say it over and over in the Bible—He will cause us to prosper in spite of our circumstances when we follow Him. Here is one way that I agree with God that I am blessed:

Lord, thank You that I have been blessed with all spiritual blessings in the heavenly places in Christ Jesus. Thank You for loving me. I am blessed. You have rescued me from the curse and given me a new blessed life. Thank You that You cause me to prosper in all good things. Thank You that You have good plans for me. Thank You that You not only take pleasure in causing me to prosper, but You take pleasure in me!

God's blessing comes with a purpose that goes far beyond us. Good parents teach their children to share. How much more does our Father want us to share Christ and all of His goodness with other people?

> God blesses us,
> That all the ends of the earth may fear Him.
> (Ps. 67:7)

We aren't blessed just so we can have more. We're blessed so more people near and far can know Christ. Our blessing extends to reach the world so that people will know God.

Two of the most powerful revelations we can learn are who we are in Christ and all that He has given us. As we learn these truths, we can apply them and agree with God that they are true in our lives. Each time you come to a Scripture passage that contains a truth about your life in Christ, agree with God. Begin agreeing with Him that what He says is true about your life. You may not *feel* like what God says is true; however, your feelings do not change God's truth. Christ in you is the hope of glory—the full reality of the goodness of God in your life. Anything less is not good enough, because in Christ, you are so much better than that!

... Taking the **Next Step** ....

God wants us to know and agree with Him about who we are in Christ. The starting place is knowing what the Bible says about us and letting His image of us become our image of ourselves.

Think about It

1. When you have felt less than your true self in Christ, what has helped you to change?

2. In what ways, if any, does your inner image need to move closer to God's image of you? What would help you make the move?

3. Identify some common phrases people use that don't line up with truth in God's Word. How could these phrases be changed to agree with His truth?

4. In what practical ways does receiving God's forgiveness set you free? Think of a specific example in your life.

5. In what ways does being righteous influence your conversations with God? With other people? With your self-talk? With your actions?

Put It into Action

Identify one area of your life where you would like to exchange your self-image for God's image of you. Find and write out at least one verse of Scripture relating to what God says about you in this area. For the next week, pray about that verse, agree with God about its truth, and thank Him for it. Ask Him to renew your mind in that area.

You've Got What It Takes

Knowing What You Have in Christ

. . . .

But thanks be to God, who always leads us in triumph
in Christ.

2 Corinthians 2:14

Since I have the same last name as the author John Grisham,
I am sometimes asked if we're related. I was told a relative
traced our genealogy and said that we were indeed related.
Even though I have never met John Grisham, I like knowing the possible connection. Now when I'm asked, I'd like
to be very casual and answer, "Yes, we're distantly related."
However, I'd feel guilty for being pretentious and then have
to admit that I'd never met him.

Several years ago, I did meet the author's father, John
Grisham Sr. We shared some stories and laughs together. I
asked him if "relatives" had come out of the woodwork since
his son had become famous. He grinned and nodded yes.

As we talked, we tried to trace the possible family connection. Since I didn't know my family beyond my grandfather, I wasn't a lot of help in the hunt.

I like the thought of possibly being related to John Grisham, especially if some of the author's gene pool has splashed over into my writing ability. However, even if we were truly related, it wouldn't change who I am.

You've Got the Name

When we come to faith in Christ, we only have to trace our genealogy one generation. Spiritually, we are each first-generation descendants of Jesus. He literally *changes* our spiritual family of origin and places His Spirit in us. He elevates our position in Him to the right hand of the Father. He delegates to us the authority that He won when He defeated Satan on the cross.

We are even given His name to use, the greatest name that ever has and ever will exist. Because He humbled himself and died on a cross for us, "God exalted him to the highest place and gave him the name that is above every name" (Phil. 2:9 NIV). Imagine this verse visually represented. Write out Jesus's name, underscore it with a line, and then envision every other name in the universe below that line.

JESUS

Everything Else

Do you have anything in your life that shouts, "I'm bigger than the name of Jesus"? Whether it's addiction, grief, infertility, prison, loneliness, materialism, failure, illness, unemployment, divorce, job, brokenness, loss, sin, success, money, or something else—you fill in the blank—it's all below the line. There is nothing greater than Jesus's name, because His name carries the full weight of His authority and power.

When we come into the family of God, we are immediately one with Christ. In Him, we've got what it takes to overcome in life. However, overcoming doesn't happen automatically. We have to know and then use what He's given us. In this chapter we are going to explore several areas that make the difference between barely getting by and thriving in life. Whether you're just learning these truths or being reminded of them, Christ wants you to fully experience and live a vibrant life in Him!

You've Got Power

For almost three decades, I didn't know there was power available to help me break the cycle of spiritual defeat in my Christian life. Then my friends Jerry and Nancy started teaching me the role of the Holy Spirit. They explained that He lives in everyone who follows Christ and gives us the power we need to live purposeful and holy lives. It was a great relief to know that I didn't have to rely on my ability to live the life that Christ had given to me. Hope had arrived to help me live the life I had been given.

God isn't trying to keep His power from us; He's trying to give His power to us. He wants us to know "the surpassing greatness of His power toward us who believe" (Eph. 1:19). He wants us to be good receivers.

If we are in Christ, His Spirit lives in us. Paul writes, "Your body is a temple of the Holy Spirit who is in you" (1 Cor. 6:19). God wants to fill His temple with Himself. In fact, His desire is that we all "be filled with the Spirit" (Eph. 5:18). That means He wants each of us to *continually* be filled up with His Spirit. It is through His fullness in us that we have the power to overcome the hurdles in this life.

D. L. Moody was a great evangelist in the nineteenth century. Referring to being filled with the Holy Spirit, he once said, "I'm a leaky bucket." Moody understood his moment-by-moment need for the filling of the Spirit.

So, how do we stay filled up with the Holy Spirit? We don't have to beg or plead. Remember, it's God's idea, not ours. As we surrender ourselves to Him, we simply ask Him to fill us and then by faith we receive. Should there be anything in our lives that interrupts His flow, He will let us know. Our yielding to God is the door to His power to overcome in life. Faith is the key that opens the floodgate to receiving.

The apostle Paul asks us an interesting question: "Did you receive the Spirit by the works of the Law, or by hearing with faith?" (Gal. 3:2). The simplicity of that question reminds us that we don't earn our way to being filled with God's Spirit. The Holy Spirit is a gift and is received by trusting Him. However, we need to hear this message of truth because "faith comes from hearing, and hearing by the word of Christ" (Rom. 10:17). The process is simple: surrender and receive. Our role is receiving by faith; God's role is the filling.

> We can't round up enough containers to hold everything God generously pours into our lives through the Holy Spirit! (Rom. 5:5 Message)

His outpouring also includes spiritual gifts that we use in service in His kingdom. God has given us everything that it takes to experience life to the fullest. As Jesus said, "Walk with me and work with me—watch how I do it. Learn the unforced rhythms of grace" (Matt. 11:29 Message). We can rest step-by-step in Him and in His Word. Along the way, we will bear much fruit, and our lives will bring glory to Him. Life becomes an adventure, striving falls away, and peace replaces anxiety.

But . . . You've Got a Bully

When I was in the second grade, a girl I'll call Rachel was the tallest kid in class. She had brown hair that she pulled back in a high ponytail with bangs. She wore those brown and white saddle oxfords—the ones with the hard, orange-colored soles. One day during recess, I was on the sidewalk minding my own business. Apparently, Rachel didn't like sharing the sidewalk with me. She sized me up, tightened her lips, drew back her right saddle oxford, and nailed it into my shin. From that point forward, as far as I was concerned, Rachel ruled recess.

We probably all remember a childhood bully. A lot of things don't change. Today, there is a bully who stalks us all the time, trying to control what doesn't belong to him. However, we are privy to his tactics.

> Be of sober spirit, be on the alert. Your adversary, the devil, prowls around like a roaring lion, seeking someone to devour. But resist him, firm in your faith. (1 Peter 5:8–9)

That bully has been luring people into his bully web of deception ever since his first conversation with Eve. God gave Adam and Eve and their offspring authority to rule the earth. Then the devil came on the scene. It started off with a seemingly innocent question: "Indeed, has God said, 'You shall not eat from any tree of the garden'?" (Gen. 3:1). No big deal. Or was it?

From the very beginning the enemy used the same ploy that he still trots out today: he questions and contradicts God's Word.

> The serpent said to the woman, "You surely will not die! For God knows that in the day you eat from it your eyes will be opened, and you will be like God, knowing good and evil." (Gen. 3:4–5)

Their conversation quickly escalated to Eve being deceived and caving in to temptation. Adam chose to sin and lost the authority that God had given them to rule over the earth. Big trouble!

You've Got Authority

The day came when the bully had another conversation. This time he was in a face-off with Jesus. After Jesus spent forty days in the wilderness, Satan came and tempted Him to sin. The devil used his same old ploy. He twisted the Word of God to try and manipulate Jesus into sinning. However, Jesus responded to the devil by accurately using God's Word against him. Match over! The bully skulked away (Matt. 4:1–11).

Bullies don't give up easily. Later, there was a showdown of eternal proportions. Blood was shed. There was a cross, death, and darkness. It looked like the devil had won again. Or had he? What appeared to be defeat was in fact our victory. Jesus rose from the dead, having conquered death, hell, and the devil. He took back the authority that the devil had stolen from Adam.

> When He had disarmed the rulers and authorities, He made a public display of them, having triumphed over them through Him. (Col. 2:15)

Forty days later, Jesus told his disciples, including you and me, that all authority in both heaven and earth had been given to Him. On the heels of that revelation He commissioned us, "Go therefore and make disciples of all the nations" (Matt. 28:19).

Jesus holds both authority and power. Authority without power is impotent. We see this regularly in the news. If a leader has authority but doesn't have power, that leader can't fend off the enemy. At the same time, power without authority can be anarchy. It takes both authority and power for legal rule.

Just before Jesus ascended back to heaven, He promised, "But you will receive power when the Holy Spirit comes on you; and you will be my witnesses" (Acts 1:8 NIV). He not only gave us authority to go in His behalf, but He also promised us the power of His Holy Spirit. We need both His authority and His power to fulfill God's purpose in our lives.

The plot thickens. It gets even better! Jesus returned to heaven, and He sat down at the right hand of the Father, "far above all rule and authority and power and dominion, and every name that is named, not only in this age but also in the one to come" (Eph. 1:21). Jesus won back our spiritual authority over the enemy and then returned to His position in heaven as the all-powerful ruler. Just so there wouldn't be any question about Jesus's scope of authority, the next couple of verses in the passage make His reign very clear: "And He put all things in subjection under His feet, and gave Him as head over all things to the church, which is His body, the fullness of Him who fills all in all" (1:22–23). Most of us know that Jesus is the head of the church. We also know that the church is His body here on earth. Jesus delegated His authority to the church to do His work on earth.

Until the day when the enemy is permanently banished from the world, there will be spiritual battles. However, Christ came and destroyed the enemy's work. "The Son of God appeared for this purpose, to destroy the works of the devil" (1 John 3:8). Jesus's reason for coming was to overcome the enemy to deliver us from his authority and power. "You know of Jesus of Nazareth, how God anointed Him with the Holy Spirit and with power, and how He went about doing good and healing all who were oppressed by the devil, for God was with Him" (Acts 10:38). When He was here He defeated the enemy.

Jesus made a clear distinction between what the devil does and what He does: "A thief is only there to steal and kill and destroy. I came so they can have real and eternal life, more and better life than they ever dreamed of" (John 10:10 Message). Like a bully, the devil takes what doesn't belong to him. He brings death in place of life and causes devastation. Jesus has given us His name, His Word, the power of His Holy Spirit, and His authority to enable us to win our spiritual battles. He has also given us spiritual protection against the wiles of the bully.

You've Got Armor

In the small Southern town where I grew up, basketball was the main event. On the weekends during basketball season, almost everyone came out to see the girls' games, followed by the boys' games. Our little gym would be packed with parents, neighbors, and the community as they cheered us on. I loved to suit up in my satiny red and white uniform, complete with white Converse high tops, and run out onto the court. I would have never considered facing an opponent without having on my uniform.

God has given us a spiritual suit of armor. We need to stay suited up and ready. It's our protection from the enemy, and it enables us to win over him.

> Finally, be strong in the Lord and in his mighty power. Put on the full armor of God, so that you can take your stand against the devil's schemes. For our struggle is not against flesh and blood, but against the rulers, against the authorities, against the powers of this dark world and against the spiritual forces of evil in the heavenly realms. (Eph. 6:10–12 NIV)

It is sometimes easy to forget that the devil is looking to harm us. He's on the prowl to attack, plunder, and destroy lives. We're prone to look at unusual struggles and try to fix them or to better control our circumstances. But often nothing seems to work. The onslaught gains momentum. Then we remember that an unseen battle rages around us. This is no game. There is an active enemy in our midst. We need all that God has given us to win against his schemes.

A friend who led a large Bible study in Milwaukee shared that a retired CEO once demonstrated to the group how he put on the spiritual armor. Every morning for many years, this prominent businessman and his wife started the day by getting dressed spiritually. As they sat on the side of the bed, they didn't just say, "I put on the helmet of salvation." They used Scriptures to attach every piece of armor to their union with Jesus. They acknowledged *Him* as their protector. Their practical application put a fresh perspective on Paul's instructions to "put on the Lord Jesus Christ" (Rom. 13:14).

To make the armor easier to remember, we can start at the top of our head and move down through each piece. Here is a brief overview of how we might "put on" the armor of God as described in Ephesians 6.

- Lord, I put on the helmet of salvation. "Salvation is found in no one else, for there is no other name under heaven given to mankind by which we must be saved" (Acts 4:12 NIV). Jesus, You are my salvation. Thank you!

- I put on the breastplate of righteousness. "He made Him who knew no sin to be sin on our behalf, so that we might become the righteousness of God in Him" (2 Cor. 5:21). Jesus, You are my righteousness. I purpose to walk in Your righteousness today.

- I buckle the belt of truth around my waist. Jesus, You said, "I am the way, and the truth, and the life" (John 14:6). You are the truth. I purpose to speak and live in Your truth today.

- I outfit my feet with the readiness of the gospel of peace. Jesus, You are the good news of my peace with God, "having made peace through the blood of [Your] cross" (Col. 1:20). You always stand ready for all things. I walk in Your readiness and peace.

- I take up the shield of faith to extinguish every fiery dart of the enemy. I lock my eyes on Jesus, "the pioneer and perfecter of faith" (Heb. 12:2 NIV). Jesus, You started and are developing my faith. My trust in You quenches every fiery dart of the devil.

- I take up the sword of the Spirit, which is the Word of God. Jesus, You are the living Word who "became flesh and made [Your] dwelling among us" (John 1:14 NIV). I use Your Word against the enemy to defeat him.

- I stay in constant communication with You—with all kinds of prayer and petitions, praying at all times in the Spirit—keeping alert (Eph. 6:18).
- I put on the Lord Jesus Christ (Rom. 13:14). You are in me and my life is hidden in You (Col. 3:3). I receive You as my protector, power, and authority over the enemy.

How does this practically apply in our lives? Recently, I felt like I had fallen into a spiritual hornet's nest. It seemed like the more I tried to do the right thing, the more of a mess things became. I realized that there seemed to be much more going on than what was visible. I stopped and turned my attention to Christ and suited up in His armor.

I prayed, thanking God that Jesus was my protection. Piece by piece, I "put on" the Lord Jesus Christ—all that He had given to protect me and to equip me. With my focus and confidence in Christ, I agreed with Him that, "Jesus, You are my salvation, righteousness, peace, the author and completer of my faith, and the living Word of God, which is my weapon against the enemy. I suit up in You, I submit to You, and I overcome in Your name!"

There was a shift that took place in me as I put on my spiritual protection. I became aware of *whose* I am and of *who* I am in Christ. By the grace of God, I landed on my feet and made it through stronger and wiser. The enemy's plots are no match for Jesus's power and protection in our lives.

You've Got to Submit to Resist

How else do we practically apply our position in Christ when the enemy attacks? Here is our first line of defense: "Submit yourselves, then, to God. Resist the devil, and he will flee from you" (James 4:7 NIV). Submission enables us to accept all that God provides. If we're holding back and trying to maintain control, we're vulnerable. As we yield to Him,

Christ's authority is over, under, and around us. As we draw near, He draws near to us.

After we have submitted to God, *then* we resist the devil. We resist him the same way that Jesus did, by standing firm and using God's Word to defeat him.

As an example, when I went through a season of financial struggle, I submitted to the authority of God's Word over my life and circumstances. I would privately declare and pray Scripture out loud:

No weapon formed against me will prosper (Isa. 54:17).

Lord, You provide all my needs according to Your riches in Christ Jesus (Phil. 4:19).

I am seated in the heavenly places in Christ Jesus (Eph. 2:6), and You are my wisdom, my righteousness (1 Cor. 1:30), and my peace. In You I am overwhelmingly more than a conqueror (Rom. 8:37).

Fully submitted to God, I stood on His Word, spoke it, and resisted the enemy. Then peace came to me. It took time for the situation to change. However, God was faithful to always provide for me and to help me grow in trusting Him.

As we submit to God, our shield of faith is our defense force against the enemy's attacks. It will protect our spiritual shins and everything else. Our faith in God will extinguish the fiery missiles that are sent against us. We maintain absolute confidence in the Greater One, "For whatever is born of God overcomes the world; and this is the victory that has overcome the world—our faith" (1 John 5:4). Hold tightly to your shield of faith!

We resist the devil by using our spiritual sword—God's Word. Its power is beyond our comprehension. His angels act on His Word. They are "mighty in strength, who perform His word, obeying the voice of His word!" (Ps. 103:20). In the spiritual realm, the angels are responding to His Word.

This gives us another reason to agree with God's Word and to speak His truth over our lives.

When the enemy is trying to bully his way into your life—appearing as an angel of light and luring you into temptation, deception, discouragement, doubt, calamity, or anything else—you can say with certainty, "Father, I submit myself to You. I resist the devil. I thank You that he has to leave. In Jesus's name." Stay yielded to Him and keep your confidence in His Word and His faithfulness—the enemy has to run.

You Have Everything You Need

When I read C. S. Lewis's book, *The Lion, the Witch and the Wardrobe*, I didn't want it to end. It was one of those books that captivated my interest. Lewis made Aslan, the lion that represents Christ, so real that I saw in new ways the kindness, power, and love of Jesus. When Aslan was put to death in the book, I didn't want him to die. However, when he came back to life, I reveled in the reminder that the enemy is defeated and Jesus indeed reigns.

The book ended, but the real battle continues. We often sense that there is an evil vortex working to suck us into it. Sometimes, however, the battle is against our own flesh. As the cartoon character Pogo stated so well, "We have met the enemy and he is us."

Christ empowers us to walk with Him in every area of our lives. We are able to obey Him in our thoughts, motives, emotions, and actions. He gives us the fruit of the Spirit, which is "love, joy, peace, forbearance, kindness, goodness, faithfulness, gentleness and self-control" (Gal. 5:22–23 NIV). We have everything that we need to live the life that He has given us. We do not have to endure defeat in any area of our lives.

A young woman once asked me to help her in an area where she struggled. What she needed to do seemed so obvious to me.

While we were talking on the phone, I suddenly sensed God's whisper, "When are you going to stop overeating?"

I thought, "What? We're working on her." But God was dealing with me and my choices!

Overeating and eating the wrong kinds of foods were things that God had been working on with me. Often I'd feel guilty, take a stab at changing my eating habits, try harder, only to fail again and repeat the cycle. Then I would try to avoid the issue with God or change the subject, as though He might not notice.

As I got off the phone, God brought the truths that I had been trying to share with this young woman right back to apply in my own life. And I got it. He also reminded me to get the log out of my own eye. I told God I had tried and failed so often in controlling my appetite. I desperately needed His help. I asked for His grace to succeed in this area of my life.

That day, I fully surrendered my eating habits to God. I asked Him to give me the power and ability to change. He has and continues to help me in this lifestyle change. It's not always easy. At times I still fail and overeat unhealthy things, but it is different now. I'm quick to turn to Him, talk to Him about it, and get back on track. He wants me to live healthy, and I've got to work with Him, not against Him. He's given me the ongoing power to make and follow right choices in an area that had been a huge stumbling block in my life.

God wants full access in every area of our lives. Maybe you've been to a special event where only the important, trusted people with all-access passes were allowed backstage. God has given each of us an all-access pass to Him through Christ. However, to enjoy the full benefit of our extended privileges, we'll need to give Him all access into our lives. That means that we fully yield to and obey Him.

When we live filled with His Spirit, we can enjoy experiencing Him in every area of our lives. As we do, we will have all the power we need for all the need that we have. We can trust Him with confidence that we've got what it takes to win in life—Jesus, who always leads us in triumph (2 Cor. 2:14).

... Taking the **Next Step** ....

Knowing the power and authority that we have in Christ changes everything. We can take hold of God's spiritual provisions and stop getting trounced by the devil. In Christ we have what it takes to win in life.

Think about It

1. Is there any area of your life that shouts, "I'm bigger than the name of Jesus"? If so, in what ways is Jesus's name greater?
2. How are you yielding to or possibly hindering the power of the Holy Spirit in your life?
3. In what ways does knowing your spiritual position in Christ, in both power and authority, practically affect your life?
4. How does God's spiritual armor practically affect your everyday life?
5. Is there any area of your life that isn't fully submitted to God and that weakens your ability to resist the devil's onslaughts? If so, what are you going to do about it?
6. In what ways have you experienced God providing everything you need to overcome in an area of your life?

Put It into Action

Read back through the armor of God in Ephesians 6:10–18. Practice personalizing and putting on the armor before getting out of bed each morning this week. You may want to write it out in your own words.

Part 3

Thriving

The **Adventure** of
Life in the **Spirit**

Great Expectations

Trusting in God's Greatness

. . . .

For the eyes of the LORD move to and fro throughout the earth that He may strongly support those whose heart is completely His.

2 Chronicles 16:9

A friend recently gave me a new mouse pad for my computer. I'm using it right now as I type. When she handed it to me, she tilted her head and said, "I got this for you because it seems like life has given you a lot of Plan Bs." Then I read the words that were printed on the brightly colored pad: *Life is all about how you handle Plan B.*

While I'm not sure that my life has had any more turns than most, I understood what my friend meant. My first big Plan B was starting over as a single again. Around the same time, the corporation I worked for had a multistate merger, and I was moved from executive management back to middle management.

Life had changed at home, at work, and even socially. In a culture that's focused on families, I became very aware of losing the identity of being married. My small group at church had been for couples. Dinner out and getting together with friends had been done as couples. Now, even family holidays felt like coming home from college again. Suddenly, I felt like there wasn't a place where I really fit in.

Sometimes the life we have is very different from the life we expected. Maybe you've found yourself in a challenge that you never signed up for. Maybe you're wondering what the next season of life holds for you. We all know the anguish of watching our plans suddenly change. Those uncertain times of life come in both big and small packages. It can be tough to trust God when change collides with our plans. However, God can turn those challenges into opportunities for something far better than we had ever expected. God is the master of turning Plan Bs into A+ futures!

When life shifts, it's time to put your hope in God into high gear. Whether life knocks you down or just throws a few hurdles in your path, God is never surprised. He holds the master plan and always has your next step waiting for you.

Stop, Drop, and Roll

While we like to think we are in charge of our lives, there is actually very little we can control except ourselves and how we respond to circumstances. Challenges come to all of us. It's how we react that determines whether we will experience God and His greatness or endure the limits of our own smallness. Throughout the Bible we see how men, women, and even nations rallied in the face of difficulty. Some turned and ran to God; others ran away.

God knows how to turn challenges into defining moments of destiny. Scripture tells the story of one man who led a nation to expect great things from God. Jehoshaphat was the leader of Judah, God's people. He woke up one morning and had no idea that life was about to serve up a Plan B. It's sometimes like that; one minute everything is fine, and the next minute everything changes. How he responded in these surprising circumstances set the course for experiencing God's success.

One day Jehoshaphat's men rushed to tell him that the enemy was bearing down on them for battle. An unprovoked attack would soon be unleashed. Jehoshaphat responded like most people would: "Jehoshaphat was afraid" (2 Chron. 20:3). Aren't you glad that the Bible tells us how great leaders feel in crisis? They feel like we feel. It's what Jehoshaphat did with his feelings that made a difference.

Jehoshaphat took his fear and ran to the right place. He turned to God. He didn't wring his hands and start saying, "It's all over! We'll never beat this enemy." No, the Bible tells us that he "turned his attention to seek the LORD" (2 Chron. 20:3). There are times in our lives when we need to run straight to God. We don't need to throw back a few beers, take a pill, call a friend, curse, blame somebody, or hope the problem goes away. We need to do one thing only—*seek God*.

You've probably heard the saying that if you ever catch on fire you need to immediately "stop, drop, and roll." That's also good advice if the enemy is circling for the kill.

1. Stop what you're doing.
2. Drop everything and seek God.
3. Roll the problem over onto Him.

Then add one more step:

4. Do whatever God says to do. If He is silent, be patient and wait for His direction.

Sometimes the most obvious thing that needs to be done is the last thing that we do. The battle Judah faced was so critical that everything else came to a halt as they cried out to God. What Jehoshaphat did next reveals the seriousness of his desire to hear from God. He called for a fast and prayed.

Life in the Fast Lane

I've often wondered why a "fast" is not called a "slow." If you like food as much as I do, the time doesn't go fast enough. In full disclosure, I have to admit that I don't like to fast. That said, I do like the benefits that fasting can bring—the big one being hearing God more clearly. If you sort of feel like I do about fasting, you might want to keep reading.

Sometimes the difficulties we're in, like the one that Jehoshaphat faced, are so great that we can totally lose our appetites. Fasting is easier on those days. At other times just hearing a dog eat dry food can feel like torture. Even when we read the Bible, it seems like every page is talking about bread, fish, wine, and feasts!

When I was in graduate school, John, one of my good friends, started a day of prayer and fasting for the college. He wanted us to come together to seek God. I had fasted before in really serious situations but never just to listen for God's voice.

The big day came, complete with special prayer, worship, and focus on God. I did not want to fast. Instead, I went into downtown Chicago to a favorite little coffee shop for a latte and a freshly baked snickerdoodle cookie. I can still feel the texture and crumble of that cookie as I bit into it, with those little sprinkles of sugar and cinnamon on top.

That evening, I drove about an hour away from campus to hear author Jill Briscoe speak. After she taught, there was a Q&A time with her. I jumped at the opportunity to gain wisdom from this woman. I was the first one to raise my hand. Then I asked my smart question, "What would be one thing that you could tell us that would help keep our time with God fresh?"

She answered in one word, "Fasting."

Busted.

Unaware of what was going on at our campus, Briscoe went on to say that there are some things that God only reveals through fasting. She told me to read the chapter on fasting in Richard Foster's book *Celebration of Discipline*. She even told me to go to the church bookstore that night and buy it. Not only was I caught, but God had also assigned me extra reading!

I got the book that night, went home, and read the chapter. It changed my view of fasting. Foster writes,

> More than any other discipline, fasting reveals the things that control us. This is a wonderful benefit to the true disciple who longs to be transformed into the image of Jesus Christ. We cover up what is inside us with food and other good things, but in fasting these things surface. . . . Anger, bitterness, jealousy, strife, fear—if they are within us, they will surface during fasting.[1]

Now, instead of trying to get something from God, I see fasting as a way to narrow my focus to seek Him, hear what He wants to say, and become more like Him.

Sometime after I had joined the staff of Elmbrook Church, where Stuart Briscoe was senior pastor, Jill told me she remembered that night. She said she was often asked that same question. However, she remembered that night because it was the first time she had ever answered the question with "fasting." God knows how to get our attention.

The enemy and our bodies will try to talk us out of fasting with all kinds of excuses: "You've got to exercise and need nourishment." "Aren't you being a little legalistic?" "How can depriving yourself of food help you hear God better?" "Is one cookie going to stop God from talking to you?" The list goes on and on. It's an indication of just how powerfully our body opposes our spirit having control over it—which is another reason to fast. The fact is some things only happen with fasting.

Jesus told his disciples, "*Whenever* you fast . . ." (Matt. 6:16 emphasis added). He could have said just as easily, "*If* you fast . . ." So it's a reasonable conclusion that fasting is expected to be part of our lifestyle. Richard Foster writes, "Fasting reminds us that we are sustained 'by every word that proceeds from the mouth of God' (Matt. 4:4)."[2] He points us to Jesus's words, "My food is to do the will of Him who sent Me and to accomplish His work" (John 4:34). When we fast we can expect to experience an awareness of God's presence, especially as He speaks to us through His Word. To echo Jill Briscoe's wisdom, get *Celebration of Discipline*, read the chapter on fasting—and see what God will do.

Talking with God

Jehoshaphat and the whole nation of Judah were devoted to hearing God, even to the point of fasting and prayer—and they got results. We'll take a look at their prayer. But first, let's take a look at three prayer approaches that many of us cycle through. Of course, there are no "pull this lever" formulas to answered prayer. Prayer engages us with God not only to tell Him what is on our hearts but also to hear what He is saying to us.

Here's My Order

In this style of prayer, we approach God in the same way we would place our order at a drive-through window. We don't want to chitchat, we're not there for the relationship. *Get the order right. Give me what I want. I'm good to go.* We are busy people and sometimes prayer is just one more task to check off our to-do list to try to get what we want.

Formula 1 Prayer

Like a high-speed race car, this is the prayer that we sometimes think will get us where we want to go—fast. We may have learned a formula that says we need to begin prayer with worship. It is good to start there. Then we're supposed to confess to God the bad things we've done. This is good too. However, if our motive in saying these things is just to get through the formula so we can ask for the goods, then we are missing the point. Next, we quickly switch lanes to get into the reason we really came—telling God what we want Him to do for us. Have you ever felt like you were supposed to play up to God before you ask Him for something? Have you ever done it and felt like a hypocrite? Me too. God doesn't answer formulas. He answers His children who pray with confidence in Him.

Problem Prayer

Sometimes we come to God and tell Him our problem in great detail over and over and over. We often toss in multiple scenarios of what could happen if He doesn't come through for us. We usually couple these "problem prayers" with giving Him several ideas of how He could fix things for us. We bundle it all up with a lot of fear, anxiety, and worry, which eventually ends in begging. "Don't think you're going to get anything from the Master that way" (James 1:7 Message). It is the prayer of faith without doubting that God answers (James 1:6). Begging is the default mode for a lot of people when they really get serious about prayer.

What is the difference between begging and persistence? Begging comes from thinking we can eventually talk God into doing things our way or giving us what we want. It places confidence in the asking. Persistence is anchored in sustained faith over a period of time. It places our confidence in a good God with whom we have a personal relationship.

Jesus said that we won't be heard for our many words (Matt. 6:7). We're not working with a lot of faith when we beg over and over again. God says to come to His throne of grace with confidence and boldness—He doesn't say with begging—to receive mercy and grace from Him when we need it (Heb. 4:16).

Why is prayer sometimes so confusing? Who hasn't thought, "Just tell me what to do and I'll do it?" Fortunately, we can break old cycles of prayer and start fresh, *expecting* to hear answers from our great God. Prayer is about connecting with God. He understands we often don't know how to pray. He sends His Spirit to help us and intercede for us. His role is to help us pray so that we hear Him. Helping us is His idea. Our role is coming to Him and listening for Him, confident that He answers us in His love and wisdom.

Jehoshaphat's Prayer

Thankfully, on the morning that the enemy drew down on Judah, Jehoshaphat didn't try to figure out which prayer lever to pull. He had a relationship with God. He was in trouble, so he went to the one who loved him most and talked to Him. Prayer is that simple—talking with the one who loves you most and listening to Him.

As we look at Jehoshaphat's prayer, we can see some of the same elements as the above prayers. That's one reason that prayer can feel so frustrating at times—we want to "get it right" so God will answer us. However, deep down we intuitively know that it isn't about dialing in the right formula.

Jehoshaphat's approach reveals a lot about his heart. Here is a man who is truly seeking God and has complete confidence that God will respond. God is always looking at the heart, no matter how we pray. He is always looking for hearts that are looking for Him.

For the eyes of the LORD run to and fro throughout the whole earth, to show Himself strong on behalf of those whose heart is loyal to Him. (2 Chron. 16:9 NKJV)

Jehoshaphat was a man whose heart was wholly devoted to God. His prayer in 2 Chronicles 20 gives us insight into his process of seeking God, and it contains five principles that will guide us as we seek Him.

1. Declare God's Greatness (20:6)

As Jehoshaphat addresses God, he begins by focusing on God's greatness. There are four declarations that he calls out to God in prayer:

- You are the God in the heavens.
- You are Ruler over all.
- All power and might are in Your hand.
- No one can stand against God.

We honor God when we come to Him by first looking at His greatness. We bow before Him and declare that He is the only all-powerful God of the universe. However, we must never do this with a schmoozing attitude. Sometimes I catch myself doing this. I have to stop and say, "God, I'm trying to play up to You to get what I want. Will You please forgive me, change my heart, and help me?" When you sense you're in schmooze mode, that's all you've got to do. Call it what it is and ask for forgiveness and help—receive it, then move on.

When we are rightly aligned with God, it's so much easier to become aware of His greatness. When we see God for who He is and what He has, it builds our confidence in Him. This is the almighty One who comes to our aid when we are in need. As we focus on His power and might, it brings our problems into perspective.

One of the enemy's greatest ploys against bold prayer is shame and false guilt. We can't come with confidence to God's throne if shame is dragging us down. Often we will be tempted to confess old sins that have already been dealt with and forgiven.

> Therefore let us draw near with confidence to the throne of grace, so that we may receive mercy and find grace to help in time of need. (Heb. 4:16)

Bold prayer does not drag up forgiven sins. If that starts happening, nip it in the bud. Thank Jesus for His forgiveness, His work of mercy on the cross, and move on by focusing on God's greatness. We can't think about our past and focus on God. Let Jesus hold you up and usher you into the throne room. He loves taking you to the Father!

Remembering God's greatness puts our problems in the right perspective. He's bigger than disaster, addictions, mistakes, abuse, fears, lust, immorality, jail, disease, discouragement, depression, death, and any other troubles we may face. These are all reasons to run to God, not to stand at a distance from Him. Instead of focusing on how great your problem is, declare the greatness of God.

2. Recall God's Faithfulness (20:7-9)

Jehoshaphat recalls how God had driven out the enemy in the past. One of the strongest encouragements you can tap into is remembering how faithful God has been to you—even if your life has been hard. Where have you seen God's faithfulness to you? How has God come to your aid in the past? Where has He given you favor, gotten you through a hard place, or rescued you from a crisis? How many times has He healed you in the past? Where has He helped you do something that you didn't think you could do? We can remember all the times that we survived to have more good days, to experience more love, to eat another meal, and to make it through one more night. God is so faithful to us. He will never act outside of His faithful character. You're able to read this today only because God has been faithful to get you this far in life.

When we face difficulty, we will either look to God or stare at the problem and our inadequacies in handling it. Recently, I was facing a situation that took my emotions on a fast roller coaster. I didn't know what to do. Then I started thanking God one by one for specific ways He had helped, delivered, provided, and cared for me over the years. It was a very long list. The more I thanked Him, the more I could see His faithfulness was greater than my challenge. Recalling God's faithfulness builds our faith because we know He never changes.

Jehoshaphat not only declares God's faithfulness to his own generation, he recalls it from past generations. Then he says, "We will stand before this house and before You (for Your name is in this house) and cry to You in our distress, and You will hear and deliver us" (2 Chron. 20:9). He is determined and confident that God hears and will help them. When God's people cry out to Him, He listens and answers.

3. Ask God for His Help (20:11-13)

Finally, Jehoshaphat brings the problem to God in faith and asks for His help, fully expecting Him to answer. Was God going to be more open to the people's request because they had spent time declaring His character? No. Rather, focusing on God builds faith, brings perspective, and prepares our hearts. "Faith comes by hearing, and hearing by the word of God" (Rom. 10:17 NKJV). They had a big request, and they needed to bring it to Him with absolute confidence that He would help them.

4. Acknowledge You're Powerless (20:12)

As the enemy approached, Jehoshaphat realized, "We are powerless before this great multitude . . . nor do we know what to do." We've all been to the place where there are no options available to us but God. We know that our options are limited because we've often been looking for ways other than God. We simply need to admit that we are powerless. He knows it. We need His help and can expect Him to come through. There is humility in admitting our powerlessness that opens the door for God's work and power to flow into our lives (James 4:6).

5. Keep Your Eyes on God (20:12)

Jehoshaphat then says, "Our eyes are on You." When we are powerless and stuck, there is only one right place to look. All power and might are in God's hand (2 Chron. 20:6). Where else are you going to go? The One who has all power is also the One who has your solution.

We will never have a problem that is beyond God's reach. That doesn't mean that everything turns out the way that we think it should. It does mean that we can trust Him to help us. We can be confident that the ultimate outcome will be for our good and His greater good. We can rest secure, expecting Him to answer.

Answered Prayers

In a world where we're used to instant gratification, sometimes this want-it-now mindset trickles into our prayer lives. When Jehoshaphat called on God, He answered immediately. Sometimes God does act swiftly. Other times we wonder why it takes so long. Either way, it's never too long to wait on God.

The words that God spoke to Jehoshaphat and the people of Judah are timeless and apply to you and me: "Do not fear or be dismayed because of this great multitude, for the battle is not yours but God's (2 Chron. 20:15).

- Do not fear.
- Do not be dismayed.
- The battle is not yours but God's.

Over and over in the Scriptures we are told not to be afraid. When we are trusting God, there is never a reason to be overcome by fear or disillusionment. We can take our emotions to God. Given free rein, feelings will hijack our faith. God knows how to take care of us. He wants us to keep our focus on Him, not on the difficulty or on our feelings.

Judah was then given a powerful message of hope: "the battle is not yours but God's." The only thing they had to do was face the enemy in faith, trusting God to fight on their behalf. As they kept their confidence in Him and obeyed Him, the enemy crumbled before their eyes. God miraculously delivered an entire nation.

Sometimes God calls us to stand and watch Him defeat the enemy. Other times there is a battle to fight. At all times our position is a place of rest, leaning on Him to do the impossible. Our battle is His battle. While He may not lead us the same way each time, He always has a way to carry us through the challenges of life. Our role is to remain with Him each step of the way.

Expect the Greatness of God

When we remember that the real battle is fought in the spiritual arena, it is easier to believe that the battle is God's. Throughout the Bible, God has given His people unique plans for victory. Seldom did they look like the strategies that we would have developed, because His ways are so much greater.

> For My thoughts are not your thoughts,
> Nor are your ways My ways," declares the LORD.
> "For as the heavens are higher than the earth,
> So are My ways higher than your ways
> And My thoughts than your thoughts." (Isa. 55:8–9)

Let's look at several creative ways God has worked in the lives of His people. His hand is never too short to save. He knows when and how to deliver us. Being reminded of His faithfulness and creative solutions can be a great encouragement to our faith.

Horns and Marches

God told Joshua that His people were to march around the city of Jericho for seven days and then blow trumpets. Together they followed His directions, even though it sounded ridiculous. They marched and blew their trumpets, and God did the impossible. God is not limited by circumstances. Never be tricked into thinking that your situation is too difficult for God.

Fire Walking

Because they would not deny God by bowing to the king, Daniel's friends, Shadrach, Meshach, and Abednego, were bound and tossed into a furnace fired up seven times hotter than normal. Three men went into the furnace, but four men walked in the fire. The Lord was with them. I'm pretty certain they weren't walking and talking about how powerful the king was who threw them into the furnace! The three came out without even the smell of smoke on their clothes. As a result, the king declared, "There is no other god who is able to deliver in this way" (Dan. 3:29). God knows how to help you when the heat is on!

Hungry Lions

When you think you're having a rough run of things, remember Daniel. The king punished him by trying to make him a meal for the lions. But God shut the chops of those big cats. Consequently, God turned the heart of another king who then decreed that his kingdom would fear God. He can shut the enemy's mouth and turn the heart of kings like rivers in the palm of His hand (Prov. 21:1).

A Rock

David was just a kid on a food delivery when he collided with destiny. Suddenly face-to-face with the enemy, courage rolled off his lips: "I come to you in the name of the LORD of hosts, the God of the armies of Israel . . . that all the earth may know that there is a God in Israel, and that . . . the LORD does not deliver by sword or by spear; for the battle is the LORD's and He will give you into our hands" (1 Sam. 17:45–47). David cut off the head of Goliath that day and took a step toward becoming the king of Israel. Only God! He knows how to deliver and bless you.

A Raised Staff

God's people were escaping the tyranny of a cruel slave master who ruled Egypt. They had no hope but God. "Do not fear!" Moses encouraged them. "Stand by and see the salvation of the LORD which He will accomplish for you today. . . . The LORD will fight for you while you keep silent" (Exod. 14:13–14). Moses then lifted his staff, and God parted the water, saved His people, and killed the enemy. God knows how to carry you over or through the torrents of life.

The Cross

Jesus did nothing wrong, but He took all wrong upon Himself. Wicked men crucified Him on a cross and buried Him. But death could not overcome Life Himself. He came out of that grave. God had a greater plan that included you and me! There is no problem, no enemy stronger than our God.

Whatever you are walking through today, God has a bigger purpose. He knows how to bring you through. It may not look like what you expect, because God has a greater plan. We can't see the whole picture now, so we're tempted to think too small about a big God.

Nothing boxes in God. We are limited in ourselves, but we're completely unlimited in Him. Our resources are beyond the practical and natural. They are held in a supernatural God. He wants to show us "the surpassing greatness of His power toward us who believe" (Eph. 1:19). He's looking all over right now to strongly support people whose hearts are completely His (2 Chron. 16:9).

...Taking the **Next Step** ....

There are times in all of our lives when we feel the full attack of living in a broken world. These battles give us the opportunity to see the greatness of God and to trust Him to do what only He can do.

Think about It

1. In what ways are you currently expecting to see God's greatness in your life?
2. In the last twenty-four hours, how has God's greatness influenced your life?
3. Think of a specific time when God's faithfulness amazed you. How did it affect your relationship with Him?
4. When you are in a crisis, what helps you focus on God's greatness instead of on the problem?
5. When you are faced with a challenge, what helps you keep your confidence in God?

Put It into Action

God is looking for people He can strongly support. The criteria is having a heart that is completely His. Spend some time in conversation with Him about being one of those people.

Saying No to Fear

Having Faith in God When You Feel Afraid

. . . .

> For God has not given us a spirit of fear, but of power and of love and of a sound mind.
>
> 2 Timothy 1:7 NKJV

There was a time when fear seldom registered on my radar. However, the more I moved forward in trusting God, the more I was taunted by it. One day, while out for an early morning walk, it suddenly dawned on me how fear had gradually colored my thinking a murky gray. One by one, I sensed God showing me how the "what ifs" were draining the joy right out of my life.

Part of a Scripture verse popped into my mind from Jesus's parable of the talents in Matthew 25: "I was afraid, and went out and . . ." However, I drew a total blank on what the man did in response to his fear. The expression *fraidy-blanks* popped into my mind for the wrong things that we're tempted to do in response to fear. I realized that I had some fraidy-blanks looming in my life.

When I got home and looked up the passage of Scripture, I read, "And I was afraid, and went away and hid your talent in the ground" (Matt. 25:25). Instead of investing what he had been given, the man squirreled it away in fear. As a result, what he had been given was taken away. He was called wicked and lazy and was cast away—all because of a fraidy-blank response.

Fraidy-blanks are based in negative "what-if" scenarios. What if something happens to my kids, marriage, health, house, finances, or job? What if God doesn't come through for me this time? Fear may shout a threat or whisper a casual thought. Either way, it can lodge an arrow of doubt in our minds. It can be completely logical or totally irrational. When fear is given ground, it can roar through our minds and drag our emotions straight into the enemy's camp. We don't have to be held captive by fear! God wants our fraidy-blanks filled with faith.

Standing Against Fear

Do you ever wonder how two people can go through the same circumstances and have opposite responses? There's a story in the Bible that shows us a couple of ways that can happen. Under Moses's leadership, twelve men were given the command to scout out the land that God had promised to give His people. When they finished forty days of spying in the new territory, this was their report:

> We went into the land to which you sent us, and it does flow with milk and honey! Here is its fruit. But the people who live there are powerful, and the cities are fortified and very large. (Num. 13:27–28 NIV)

The spies giving the report elaborated on the greatness of the enemy, and the people got stirred up.

Then Caleb silenced the people before Moses and said, "We should go up and take possession of the land, for we can certainly do it." (Num. 13:30 NIV)

Realizing the report was striking fear in the people, Caleb had tried to calm them and assure them of their victory.

But the men who had gone up with him said, "We can't attack those people; they are stronger than we are. . . . We seemed like grasshoppers in our own eyes, and we looked the same to them." (Num. 13:31, 33 NIV)

The spies didn't just give this report to Moses; they gave it to the entire nation of Israel. What happened next could only be described as a nation swallowed by terror. The people cried out, wanted to run back to slavery in Egypt, and even accused God of evil.

Joshua, one of the spies, stood up to their tirade and reminded them that God had given them this great land—the Promised Land. However, the people got stuck in fear. Instead of trusting God, they responded in anger, unbelief, and rebellion. Because of their unbelief and disobedience, God kept that whole generation out of the Promised Land, except for Joshua and Caleb.

Here were people in the crosshairs of destiny, but they allowed fear to rip God's best from their future. They had no idea that their fraidy-blank response would result in them living the rest of their lives in a desert. The people weren't wrong to feel fear, because there is no sin in feeling fear. Their disobedience came when they believed and acted on the fear instead of trusting and obeying God. Fear works to edge out faith. But faith in God is greater than fear.

If you've missed God or disobeyed Him because you've been afraid, do not fear! God is merciful. You have a Savior. Run back to Jesus. He knows how to help you move forward in trusting Him.

Choose Your Campsite Carefully

When I was a kid, we would go camping every summer on the Buffalo River in the Ozarks. As soon as we arrived, my sister and I wanted to put on our swimsuits and run down to the river. However, our parents insisted that we first scout the park to find the best campsite. When we found it, we set up the tent, got everything in order, blew up our rafts, and then went swimming. We chose our campsite carefully because it was the headquarters of our entire experience.

The twelve scouts Moses sent out all experienced the same circumstances, but they camped in two different places. Ten camped in fear. Only two, Joshua and Caleb, camped in faith. Ten saw problems; two saw opportunity. Fear saw giants; faith saw God's promises. Fear saw grasshoppers; faith saw God's ability. Ten bowed to unbelief, but two bowed to God. All twelve men walked through the same fear-inducing circumstances, but each man *chose* where he would set up camp.

In the same way, where we choose to set up camp determines whether we will miss out or experience God's best for our lives. Circumstances don't control our responses—our choices do.

Three Grids of Perspective

In the story of the twelve scouts, how they viewed their circumstances, themselves, and God determined how they chose to respond. Their three viewpoints can help us evaluate how we respond to life's challenges.

The Giant Grid

Ten leaders locked their eyes on the giants. When we are looking at life through the giant grid, all we see are the problems, circumstances, and outside forces. Our view of God becomes blocked. It's like looking at the sunrise but putting your hand in front of your eyes. No matter how great the horizon, all you'll see is the back of your hand. Your hand is not bigger than the dawn or stronger than the sun. It just looks bigger because it's blocking the view.

If our focus is on life's obstacles, then we are looking at life through the giant grid. We can't focus on the natural realm and expect to win spiritual battles. That doesn't mean that we deny the difficulties, but it does mean they aren't to be our focus. We lock our attention on Jesus who holds all power and might, confident that "greater is He who is in you than he who is in the world" (1 John 4:4).

God doesn't promise a problem-free life. He makes it clear that there will be giants. He promises an abundance of His ability and goodness to overcome obstacles in order to fulfill His greater kingdom purpose in our lives. Even in the face of difficulties, "God causes all things to work together for good to those who love God, to those who are called according to His purpose" (Rom. 8:28). Giants are no match for God.

The Grasshopper Grid

Ten leaders saw themselves as bugs about to be squashed by giants. Do you ever see yourself as losing even before the battle begins? Maybe you've struggled with feelings of fear or of being inadequate, helpless, marginalized, a failure, or a victim. You don't have to fear not being big enough for the battle. God in you is more than enough!

A woman once shared with me that after she was divorced she felt like she had a giant L for "loser" plastered on her forehead. She had allowed that one event to define her identity. As a result, she took on a grasshopper self-image. She assumed everyone else saw her as a grasshopper too. She focused on a lie instead of on the truth. Eventually she renewed her mind to what God said about her in his Word. As she learned her identity in Christ, she kicked that grasshopper mentality to the curb.

God's Word can expose the lies that the enemy has planted in your mind. The ten scouts were not grasshoppers; they were men called by God for a great purpose. My friend didn't have a giant *L* on her forehead; she was a woman of God, with immeasurable value. The enemy tells you that you're a grasshopper, but God calls you blessed. The enemy says you are weak, but God says, "Let the weak say, I am strong" (Joel 3:10 KJV). The enemy taunts that you'll never make it, but God says, "No weapon forged against you will prevail" (Isa. 54:17 NIV). No matter what the enemy says, God has a sure word of your adequacy in Him: "My grace is sufficient for you, for my power is made perfect in weakness" (2 Cor. 12:9).

Is there any area of your life where you have let in a grasshopper or two? Maybe it's a grasshopper of failure, addiction, race, disability, education, gender, imprisonment, or age. Maybe it's a grasshopper that says you'll never be good enough, amount to anything, reach that goal, or overcome _____ [fill in the blank]. It's a lie. Replace it with the truth of what God says about you: "I can do all things through Him who strengthens me" (Phil. 4:13). Believing anything less than that truth means there's a grasshopper hiding in your weeds.

God has taken the enemy's *L* off of your forehead. The only *L* you have is one that stands for "Loved by God." Knowing His perfect love for you drives out fear. In Him you are blessed, chosen, anointed, gifted, able, strong, courageous, and of immeasurable value. You, my friend, are vital to God's kingdom plan—and you are the only person who can be all that God has destined you to be.

The God Grid

Joshua and Caleb didn't look through the giant grid or see themselves as grasshoppers. Their eyes were fixed on God. Only God can dwarf the giants and expel the grasshoppers in our lives. Looking to Him builds our confidence in Him.

We develop our spiritual eyes to see God's perspective by knowing Him better. As we grow in knowing Him through His Word, we understand His character and nature. We begin to see things from His viewpoint. It's like putting on spiritual binoculars to see beyond the short-range challenges into the long-range benefits of His purpose.

Joshua and Caleb were able to trust that God would give them the land He had promised. It didn't matter that there were giants, that battles would be fought, or that they would have to aggressively take hold of the land God was giving them. They saw the real goal of following God, trusting Him, and fulfilling His greater purpose.

Looking at life through the God grid filters every problem, circumstance, feeling, and thought through the confidence of who God is, what He says, and the greatness of His power. Nothing is bigger than God. The closer we are to Him the greater He appears, the smaller the giants look, and the clearer we see ourselves in Christ as "more than conquerors" (Rom. 8:37 NIV).

Resisting Fear in the Spiritual Realm

This week I sat in the doctor's office awaiting results of an ugly little skin biopsy. The assistant looked at the file, paused, and then said, "I have to see the doctor. I don't know if I'm supposed to give you this." Suddenly fear swarmed my thoughts. *What if it is a melanoma? What if I have to go through chemo? What if it's too late? What if they have to amputate my leg? What if I only have six more months to live? What if . . . ?* Just a few vague words from someone looking at a medical report sent my mind into a wild overdrive.

I ran to God with my fear. "Help! You have not given us a spirit of fear, but of power and of love and of a sound mind. God help me!" As I began to pray, look to Him, and bring His Word into my situation, fearful thoughts began to be replaced with His thoughts and peace. While I waited for the results, I still felt some fear. However, I was in a place of trust, confident that God would help me no matter what. The results were benign, and I thanked God that the battle was halted.

We often think that dealing with fear is just a natural part of life. It is only natural from the standpoint of being common to all of us. The Bible says that we are in a spiritual battle: "For our struggle is not against flesh and blood, but against the rulers, against the powers, against the world forces of this darkness, against the spiritual forces of wickedness in the heavenly places" (Eph. 6:12).

When the Bible refers to a spirit of fear, it is a different fear from the automatic response system God has programmed into our bodies. If a child is about to step into oncoming traffic, our automatic response kicks in to protect the child. Contrast that with an ongoing fear parents may have that something bad is going to happen to their child. The fear that attacks our minds with the horrid what-if scenarios is not from God. Those fears are meant to take us away from God and His best. To counter this spirit of fear, God has given us a spirit "of power and of love and of a sound mind" (2 Tim. 1:7 NKJV).

Power	His Holy Spirit (Acts 1:8) and His Word (Eph. 6:17)
Love	His perfect love drives out fear (1 John 4:18)
Sound mind	The mind of Christ (1 Cor. 2:16) and a renewed mind (Rom. 12:2)

We can choose to receive and apply what He has given us. We can choose not to allow fear (anxiety, stress, dread, concern, worry) to take control of our minds. God is very present with us and has given us what we need to overcome fear. That doesn't mean we never *feel* fear. It does mean that we can choose not to let fear rule our mind, emotions, or actions. God gives us practical directions on handling our anxieties:

> Be anxious for nothing, but in everything by prayer and supplication with thanksgiving let your requests be made known to God. And the peace of God, which surpasses all comprehension, will guard your hearts and your minds in Christ Jesus. (Phil. 4:6–7)

Some of us have heard these verses so many times that we are tempted to glance over it with a nodding yawn of familiarity. The real test of knowing Scripture is whether or not we are applying it in our lives.

Don't be anxious for anything. Stop being afraid. No matter the concern, don't be anxious! Maybe you're like me and not worrying can feel irresponsible. We can change old emotional thought patterns with new healthy responses.

God tells us what not to do, what to do, and what He will do. We don't have to let our feelings and thoughts run wherever they want to take us. God has a better way for us to handle fear:

- What we are not to do: be anxious. Stop it and run to God.
- What we are to do: pray and ask for God's help, with thanksgiving.
- What God will do: put a guard of peace around our heart and mind in Christ.

Even when you feel anxious, you don't have to stay there. You can move your tent to a new campsite and ask for God's help in your difficulty. You have the power to focus on God and what His Word says. He will raise His canopy of peace over your life.

I never remember being afraid as a child when I was with my dad or mom. (I realize that wasn't true for some of you, and

I am so sorry.) Just being with either of my parents brought security. We are God's children. When fears try to carry our hearts away, "God is our refuge and strength, a very present help in trouble" (Ps. 46:1).

Closing the Door to Fear

One day, a few years ago, I felt the urge for some greasy comfort food. I went to a drive-through and bought a burger, fries, and a soda. As soon as I got my order, I realized that I had just blown $3.85 that I should not have spent. That money could have been better used, as I was in no position to waste money on junk food. I had a pity party as I ate my burger. During that season of life, I lost a lot of battles with fear and lay awake worrying many nights. It wasn't until my finances were uncertain that I realized how much money had a hold on me.

Fears have a way of exposing areas of our lives that need greater dependence on Jesus. When we can't seem to close the door on fear, we need to allow God to probe our hearts and expose any areas where we aren't fully relying on him.

You may have heard that saying, "Fear knocked on the door and faith answered." Maybe you're like me and too many times when fear knocked, feelings and reason rolled out the red carpet. When fear knocks, answer the door with God's Word. Maybe you're thinking that you don't know the Bible well enough. That's all the more reason to get into Scripture and see what it says. With a little exploration in a concordance (the Scripture reference in the back of most Bibles and online), you can look up verses on faith, courage, power, and strength. Ask God to tell you how those passages apply to your situation. Find relevant Scriptures and then pray, soak your mind in them, memorize them, and apply them to your life. You can't be passive and expect to win against fear!

God's Word is so practical. Instead of allowing our minds to run off into all kinds of what-if scenarios, He gives us direction on how to frame our thoughts for peace.

> Finally, brethren, whatever is true, whatever is honorable, whatever is right, whatever is pure, whatever is lovely, whatever is of good repute, if there is any excellence and if anything worthy of praise, dwell on these things. (Phil. 4:8)

God doesn't tell us not to be anxious and then leave it to us to figure out how to get there from here. He also tells us how to replace the anxious thoughts with right thoughts that are true, honorable, right, pure, and worthy of praise. Worry does not fit into any of those categories.

When we realize that we're worrying, we can change the direction of our thoughts. Try it next time a fear lodges in your mind. Think of something that is true, lovely, worthy of praise. You may have to refocus time and again, but you can do it! It's impossible to think worrisome and good thoughts simultaneously.

One of my friends came to talk with me when she had received a serious medical report. The doctor had examined a lump on her body that needed to be biopsied. Too many of us know the fear that a lump or a spot can bring. Fear had taken over my friend's mind. Without even thinking, I said, "Don't you know that God has not given us a spirit of fear, but of power, love, and a sound mind?"

She was a relatively new Christian and said, "No, I didn't know that, but I receive it." God gave my friend a certainty of that Scripture and its power in her life. She anchored her thoughts in knowing that God had not given her a spirit of fear. He had given her a spirit of power, love, and a sound mind.

My friend maintained God's peace through the biopsy and while waiting for tests results. She experienced a major win over fear. Thankfully, she got good results. Her response inspires me when I'm facing my own fears. God's Word is so much more powerful than ordinary words. His Word can break through the torrents of fear.

Winning the Battle of Fear

Over the course of three years, I watched my niece, my niece-in-law, and my mother face fear as they died from cancer. I battled my own fears through that journey. I've prayed and stood with friends who were battling life crises that could have swallowed them whole. Most importantly, I've seen God strengthen and sustain all of us as fear lurked in the shadows. Here are some practical things I learned as I battled fear.

Look to Jesus

One night I was awakened by a powerful worry that seemingly came out of nowhere. I kept trying to think of all the reasons I shouldn't be worried, but I was sinking fast. I realized where my thoughts were focused, and I immediately took them to Jesus. I began by softly saying His name over and over—the name that is greater than every other name. I confessed and thanked Him that He was Lord over my life, that He was in charge, and that I trusted Him. I lay there saying the name of Jesus and thanking Him for his power at work in my life and circumstances.

Jesus . . . Jesus . . . Jesus. Your name is greater than every other name. Jesus, You are Lord over my mind, body, spirit, this room, my home, finances, relationships, ministry. Jesus, You are Lord over every area of my life. Thank You that Your power is at work in my life and situation. Thank You that no weapon formed against me will prosper. Thank You that You are the Greater One and You are in me and at work in my life.

The fear left. I realize it is not always this simple. The anxiety doesn't always leave immediately, but sometimes it does. Bringing Jesus into our situation always changes things and connects us with Peace Himself. The Greater One is with us and He will always help us. Regardless of how big the issue facing you, God's name is always greater.

> Do not fear, for I am with you;
> Do not anxiously look about you, for I am your God.
> I will strengthen you, surely I will help you,
> Surely I will uphold you with My righteous right
> hand. (Isa. 41:10)

Control Your Thought Life

Fearful thoughts left unchecked can overwhelm our mind and emotions and bleed over into our actions. We can stop them before they gain momentum:

> We are destroying speculations and every lofty thing raised up against the knowledge of God, and we are taking every thought captive to the obedience of Christ. (2 Cor. 10:5)

Speculations and lofty thoughts are all those what-if scenarios that swirl around in our minds that don't line up with God's Word. By bringing our thoughts into agreement with God's Word, we bring His power to work in our lives.

Fear is rooted in the speculation that God is not enough or that He's not going to come through for us this time. In every circumstance, challenge, and problem, God is ultimately the only One who is enough. He is the only One who is all-powerful. Any thought that says otherwise needs to be kicked to the curb.

The second part of that verse tells us what to do with our thoughts: "We are taking every thought captive to the obedience of Christ." In other words, take control of your thoughts to bring them in line with God's Word. We are responsible for what we think. One fruit of the Spirit is self-control. By God's Spirit we can control our thoughts to obey Christ—just like we can control our actions. In Him we have all the power we need for all the need we have—that includes controlling our thought life.

Pray God's Word

When I became single again, a whole new pack of fears pursued me. Fears always felt bigger at night. When I went to bed, a full-scale what-if parade would try to march through my mind. Almost every night I would set up camp in Psalm 91. I would go to sleep reading and praying:

> He who dwells in the shelter of the Most High
> Will abide in the shadow of the Almighty.
> I will say to the LORD, "My refuge and my fortress,
> My God, in whom I trust!" . . .
> For He will give His angels charge concerning you,
> To guard you in all your ways. (Ps. 91:1–2, 11)

I would personalize the verses and pray them back to God. Here's an example of how I prayed:

> *Lord, I live in the shelter of You, the Most High One. I will abide in the shadow of the Almighty—in Your protection. Lord, I say to You, "You are my refuge and my fortress, my God, in whom I trust!" Thank You that Your angels guard me.*

Every night He would reassure me that He was with me, that I was going to get through this, and that He would always take care of me. I went to sleep in peace. When we face fear with God's Word, He will take us to that secret place of His peace. God says, "Do not fear. Do not be afraid." He isn't saying don't feel the emotion of fear. He is saying, "Trust me!" We can boldly say, "I fear no evil, for You are with me" (Ps. 23:4). All of Psalm 23 is about finding our peace, protection, and comfort in God through trusting Him.

When you're wrestling anxious thoughts, find passages of Scripture that draw you toward God. Then saturate yourself in those verses. Let God reveal Himself to you in ways you have never known Him. He who is peace will be your peace.

We can do the right thing even when we feel afraid. We can fill our fraidy-blanks with faith. It's called courage—that point where trust and obedience intersect.

· · · · Taking the **Next Step** ·

Fear works to edge out faith. But faith in God is greater than fear. To a great extent, our lives will be marked by our responses to fear. We can become better equipped to use the tools that Christ has provided so we will recognize and not give in to fear. We can grow in faith and conquer fear.

Think about It

1. When you are faced with a fearful situation, do you normally respond through the giant grid, the grasshopper grid, or the God grid?
2. What would help you to better face your fears through the God grid?
3. In what practical ways could you fill any fraidy-blanks with faith?
4. How have you seen your faith grow in overcoming worry?
5. In what practical ways does God's Word help you deal with stress?

Put It into Action

Write down 2 Timothy 1:7, Psalm 91:1–2, and Isaiah 26:3. Think about these passages and select at least one to memorize this week. Ask God to help you apply these verses when stress, anxiety, worry, dread, or any form of fear comes your way.

Now Is Not the Time to Quit

Lean into God's Promises

. . . .

Be strong and courageous. Do not be afraid; do not be discouraged, for the LORD your God will be with you wherever you go.

Joshua 1:9 NIV

There are two things that I completely enjoy: nature and photography. When I'm in the outdoors with a camera, I am totally happy. God's presence seems magnified when I look through the lens of my camera.

Recently, I took a course with a professional nature photographer. One afternoon, before our evening class, he had us meet at a large arboretum for a field shoot. He had gotten there early, scouted the area, and was excited to have found the perfect scene for us to photograph.

We set up our tripods right beside his. When I looked through my camera, there was absolutely nothing I wanted to photograph. All I saw was a bunch of dead grass and leafless trees. Clearly it was still winter in Chicago. In frustration, I finally asked to look through the instructor's viewfinder. Wow! The picture popped right out of the scene. He had zoomed in on the contrast, texture, color, and form—the picture within the picture. How could we look at the exact same scene and see two totally different pictures?

Where we focus determines what we see. Perspective defines experience.

Where's your focus right now? Sometimes our field of vision is so wide that we miss the real focal point. Fortunately, God helps us to narrow the view. He says that we are to fix our eyes not on what is seen, but on what is unseen, because "there's far more here than meets the eye" (2 Cor. 4:18 Message).

In the winter, anybody can see dead grass and bare trees. In the tough times of our lives, the giants are very clear to us—the problems, the challenges, our inabilities. However, when we look through the viewfinder of faith, we start to see the unseen realm where God works and we grow.

Natural sight is easy. But when a relationship grinds against us, stress pushes us to the edge, anxiety drives our thoughts, or the pressures of life pull us down, our vision can get blurred. These things are simply snapshots of our need to focus on God and not our circumstances.

Looking through the long lens of trust empowers us not to quit when God has called us to move forward in our faith. Tough times will come and our confidence in Him will be stretched. However, in Christ we have great hope!

> There's more to come: We continue to shout our praise even when we're hemmed in with troubles, because we know how troubles can develop passionate patience in us, and how that patience in turn forges the tempered steel of virtue, keeping us alert for whatever God will do next. In alert expectancy such as this, we're never left feeling shortchanged. Quite the contrary—we can't round up enough containers to hold

everything God generously pours into our lives through the Holy Spirit! (Rom. 5:3–5 Message)

The enemy tries to use problems to destroy us, weigh us down, bring discouragement, and cause us to give up. But God can take those very things that were meant for evil and use them for good (Gen. 50:20). He wants us to look to Him, believe His Word, know His power, and experience Him more intimately. Too often, we are focused on God getting us out of a tough time when we should be focusing on Him and what He is doing through the challenge.

Trusting God When It's Tough

In the fall of 2004, I was pedaling as fast as I could to finish my PhD. At the same time, I sensed God leading me to start the speaking ministry that I'm now leading. While I had budgeted my finances for that year, things had not gone as planned. With three months left before finishing my degree, the date for my next mortgage payment was approaching, and I didn't know how I would pay it. I wasn't completely broke, but I sure was scared.

One Sunday afternoon, I was on my knees crying out to God for help. My immediate need was for that mortgage payment. I got up from praying without any sense of God's answer. From an emotional point of view, I felt nothing.

The next morning, a friend called and asked me to meet her for breakfast later in the week. While we knew each other, this would be our first one-on-one meeting. During our phone conversation she asked if there would be any way that she and her husband could help me. We had not talked about my financial situation. And while everything in me wanted to scream, "Send money!" an inner whisper held me back.

My friend then told me that she and her husband had been praying and sensed they were to pay my next month's mortgage. A couple of days later, she told me they sensed

God wanted them to cover all of my living expenses for the next three months while I finished my PhD.

Only God!

Maybe you've had a time in your life when God was so visibly active that your faith soared. You prayed and—boom!—God answered. Those are great times. But what about all the other times when we journey through the land of waiting? During those treks we're tempted to bail on a dream or give up on something that's important to us. We may even wonder if we're on the right track. Those are the times we question whether we're hearing God. It's tempting to give up believing and just quit. Don't go there. There's a better way! Real faith goes the distance with God, especially in rough terrain.

As I was finishing my doctorate, I launched the speaking ministry Livin' Ignited to help people know God and experience life to the fullest. I had been speaking part-time for about ten years and felt called to do it full-time. Some businessmen heard about what I was doing and invited me to share the ministry's vision with them. During that meeting, without being asked, these men spontaneously offered to cover the first year of my salary. Only operating costs were remaining. That first year of the ministry, God stunningly confirmed my steps of faith. He opened ministry doors and provided all my financial needs.

The second year was just as amazing as the first, but in the opposite direction. As the year began, I was staring at a blank calendar. For the next six months, all I did was study the Bible, pray, and co-lead a small home Bible study. While God was providing financially, I felt confused and discouraged, and I wondered if I had misheard God.

It's so easy for us to believe God and move forward when we *see* Him actively at work. However, what about all the other times when we're trying to believe and to act in faith but God is silent? How does it affect our faith when we ask God for healing and it doesn't come as we expect? What do we do when someone we love is distant from God and seems to be moving further away? When a relationship is crumbling under our feet? When the funds for the mortgage payment *don't* arrive? What goes on in our hearts when faith runs on a rough road?

Faith sometimes requires long stretches of believing God without seeing *any* outward evidence. By definition, "faith is the substance of things hoped for, the evidence of things not seen" (Heb. 11:1 KJV). During those times of waiting, we are tempted to watch the clock. If God doesn't respond on our timeline, doubt can wedge its way into the cracks of our faith. In Hebrews 11, we are told of people who believed God and they died in their faith. Yikes! Then again, who wants to die in doubt? Not you or me! Faith goes the distance with God.

Now Is Not the Time to Quit

There are times in life when we are following God the best that we know how and things still look bleak. During these periods our faith can take us places that our natural eyes can't see.

In that second year of Livin' Ignited ministry, I was living life in the slow lane. I wondered if it was time to throw in the towel. I called a close friend who, along with her husband, led a prison ministry. They had trusted God to financially provide for them every month for twenty-five years. I had watched them live a life of faith that defied reason. I told her my saga, expecting her to reassure me that God was going to "show up" soon. Instead, my friend chuckled as she said, "Don't you know that, just like Joshua, you are going to have to *take* possession of the land? *You're* going to have to possess what God has promised you. *Now is not the time to quit.*"

Those seven words—"Now is not the time to quit"—detonated a renewed determination of faith. When I got off the phone, I went to my Bible and started studying Joshua's life. He indeed had to take possession of the Promised Land.

Even though he had to fight giants, he never gave up doing what God told him to do. What I learned through that study changed the way I view those uncertain times in life. Faith takes possession of what God has promised *before* it is visible.

Maybe you've been called to take a long walk of faith with God. Ask Him to give you fresh confidence that He is at work in your life. Now is not the time to quit or to be discouraged.

Jesus came to give us life and life more abundantly. But there are giants in the land of Christ's abundant life. We need a tenacious confidence in Him to get there from here. Just like Joshua, we will have to move forward and take hold of what God has promised us—even in the face of giants. This means we follow Christ, battle the giants in His power, and trust Him to give us His life to the fullest. It is our faith in Him that bridges the distance between where we are and what God has promised.

Relentless Confidence in God

Joshua was a man who had faithfully served under Moses's leadership. He spied out the Promised Land, saw the giants, and stood fast with Caleb to give a good report. However, the Israelites had little trust in God to defeat the giants. Because of their unbelief, the Israelites were given forty years in the desert. Joshua had done the right thing, stood firm in faith, and believed God. However, he also had to spend four decades in the desert.

Sometimes you do the right thing and you still get tossed into the penalty box. Year after year Joshua stayed the course of faith. He and Caleb would one day physically take possession of the Promised Land with a whole new generation of people. God had a lot more to do in Joshua's life. He has a lot more to do in and through your life too.

The day came when Moses died. Joshua had been tapped on the shoulder by God to lead His people into the Promised

Land. It's easy to read Joshua's story and miss the difficulty of the situation he faced. Imagine spending forty years in the desert, and then your leader and beloved mentor dies and it's time for you to rally the troops to battle the giants their parents had fled.

Those previous forty years had put a lot of wear on Joshua's eighty-year-old body. However, he didn't use age or anything else as an excuse to step away from active duty. Joshua trusted God and not himself. He set himself in agreement with God, charged forward, and never looked back. Faith keeps relentless confidence in God. You, my friend, were cut from the same fabric as Joshua!

The "Be With You" God

God is always with us when He calls us to do something that stretches our faith far beyond our abilities. Whether we face a challenging opportunity or are walking through a hard place in life, God walks with us. Joshua faced both opportunity and difficulty as he led the Israelites into the Promised Land.

Joshua led the nation into battle against the giants who were still entrenched in the land. The players may have changed but not the game. God gave Joshua the assurance that He would be with him and guaranteed his success:

> No man will be able to stand before you all the days of your life. Just as I have been with Moses, I will be with you; I will not fail you or forsake you. (Josh. 1:5)

God will never send you out alone. He always goes with you. He will be the source of your strength. He may call you to the impossible; however, in Him every challenge becomes possible. He is the "be with you" God who promises, "Never will I leave you; never will I forsake you" (Heb. 13:5 NIV). Never get detoured by feelings of loneliness or by thinking that God has bailed on you or that the task is too great. The "be with you" God is greater—look to Him!

Maybe you're thinking, "It's great that God is with me, but I want Him to do something to change my circumstances." If circumstances don't change, the biggest giant we face may be the temptation to give up on trusting God. However, our confidence needs to be anchored in Him—in His character and nature—not in our limited understanding.

When I began my personal study on Joshua, I needed my faith strengthened. In just a few days someone asked me to lead a six-week study. A few weeks later, another ministry called and invited me to teach for six weeks. We all studied Joshua! It's great when we see God act quickly. However, as you can tell from my story and Joshua's, some things take a long time, and others end differently than we had hoped. The greater point is that, regardless of timing, events, or experiences, God is always faithful (2 Tim. 2:13). *Always.*

Following God by faith is a white-knuckle adventure. It is thrilling when we can look back and see what He was doing while we were trusting Him. As Jesus said, "My Father is working until now, and I Myself am working" (John 5:17). He is always working on His great purpose in and through our lives.

When we are called to stand between the tension of what God promises and what we see, God stands with us. He brings His ability and power into our lives. This is the same one who has told us that "nothing will be impossible with God" (Luke 1:37). Sometimes we look at what's in the Bible and then we look at ourselves, forgetting that God's power is not limited to the natural realm. Jesus promises, "With people this is impossible, but with God all things are possible" (Matt. 19:26).

It Takes Courage

A few years ago, I went to South Africa on a short-term mission trip that focused on AIDS education. We visited a high school assembly that had the most energetic pep rally I've ever seen. The assembly was led by a team of young people who were dedicated to fighting AIDS through education. Through rhythmic songs, passionate stories, and practical information, the team took their prevention message to the youth. They had a colorful booklet they distributed to every student that was aptly titled "It Takes Courage." The AIDS prevention team understood firsthand the enormous amount of courage it took to resist the temptations that could lead to AIDS (when they were given a choice). Lives were at stake, the battle was fierce, and the casualties mounted every day. It takes courage to stand against short-term pleasure for long-term benefits.

Most of us probably remember times where we have seen great courage. Just last night I watched an interview of a young war hero who had saved his men at the expense of losing part of his arm. He grabbed a live grenade that exploded as he picked it up to toss away. He never quit fighting, even at great personal loss. He believed in a purpose greater than himself. His courage saved the lives of men in his unit.

Joshua was a man who was about to step into some enormous battles. I believe he felt the same way that you and I would feel. Apparently he heard the drumbeat of fear, because he was told six times to be courageous (Deut. 31:7, 8; Josh. 1:6–7, 9, 18). God told Joshua, "Have I not commanded you? Be strong and courageous! Do not tremble or be dismayed, for the LORD your God is with you wherever you go" (Josh. 1:9). God knew the fear-inducing, head-taking giants that Joshua would face. Over and over He made sure that Joshua had a mindset of courage and strength.

God didn't call Joshua to be courageous and then leave him to rely on his own strength. God gave him the key to his success over the giants. It's the same wisdom that will cause us to succeed in our lives.

This book of the law shall not depart from your mouth, but you shall meditate on it day and night, so that you may be careful to do according to all that is written in it; for then you will make your way prosperous, and then you will have success. (Josh. 1:8)

It will take courage to live the life that God has planned for you. Courage thrives on faith. Faith is anchored in God's Word. Just like Joshua, we will have to soak our minds in God's Word. If we have applied His Word in our lives, it will rise up when the time for courage is needed. It may take us time to tap into it; however, God knows how to bring us to the place He wants us to be so we can do what He is calling us to do.

Once I was looking at a large church's list of upcoming speakers. I was familiar with the first two names. They were outstanding! Both men were popular, had tremendous teaching gifts, and wrote books the rest of us read. Then I saw the next name and my heart sank—it was me. My first thought was a simple prayer, "Oh God, no!" A grasshopper mentality had swarmed my thoughts. I didn't want courage; I wanted out!

It took me about two weeks to garner enough trust in God to believe that He could use me too. I had to get my focus off of the other speakers, off of the audience, off of myself, and on to God before the courage came. A few months later when I got up to speak, I had confidence in His ability to work through me. I'd like to say the teaching was flawless. It wasn't. While speaking, my notes *and* my Bible all fell on the floor—the first and only time that had ever happened. No problem. I gathered them up and just kept teaching. The message wasn't about me!

Courage comes when God and His purpose are the main attraction. His ability is always greater than our inability.

We all need courage to stand against our giants. Where do you need courage today to trust God? Where are you tempted to bail out in the face of pressure? God calls us to be strong and courageous. He didn't leave Joshua, He didn't leave me, and He will never leave you. You can trust God every time. "Be strong in the Lord and in the strength of His might" (Eph. 6:10).

We don't have to *feel* courage to be courageous. When I need courage but can't feel it, I take my feelings and thoughts to God along these lines:

Lord, help me! I purpose to be strong and courageous. At the same time, You know what's going on in my mind and emotions. I don't see You in my circumstances, and I don't feel You in my emotions—but I don't need to. You are with me! You are at work. God, thank You that my feelings don't define Your actions. Thank You that You promised You are never going to fail me. You are my help. Nothing is impossible to You. I believe; help my unbelief! Lord, I trust You. My eyes are on You.

God wants to be our source of strength and courage. He knows every giant we will ever face. He equips us to trust Him so we can experience His greatness in our lives. As we live in the awareness that Christ lives in us, we trust His ability instead of our inability, His power instead of our impotence, His plan instead of our ideas. We can believe God will not only *be with us* but also *be who He is* and *do what He does*.

Keep Your Eye on the Purpose

A while back, I was having coffee with my friend Lisa and her husband, Drew, who is a fitness trainer. I had been slack in my workouts, so I took the opportunity to ask an expert how to get remotivated. He gave some wise advice: "You don't need to get remotivated. You need to just go do it. The value of what you're doing has to transcend what needs to be done. You've got to keep the purpose of why you exercise in front of you. When I get up at 4:30 a.m. to go to the gym to work with clients, I never want to do it. I do it because I want to provide for my family."

I thought about Drew's words for ten days or so, trying to get psyched up enough to go back into the fitness center. I had been thinking about the extra few pounds I had gained. I didn't like the way they made me look and feel. I wanted to be healthy. Then I understood what he meant when he said, "Just go do it." My desire to be lazy was overridden by my desire to be healthy. Now I'm just doing it.

There will be days when we don't feel like believing God, and we don't want to be strong, and we sure don't feel courageous. At those times, the purpose of believing God will have to transcend the obstacles in following Him. We move forward by keeping in lockstep with Him for His greater purpose. We don't have to feel motivated to be motivated. The purpose has to transcend what we feel like doing. There's a special word for this kind of ongoing motivation: perseverance.

On the days when you hear the giants roar, keep God's purpose in front of you. He will cause you to accomplish great things that you never imagined possible—for His greater kingdom purpose. The One who called you is also the One who equips you to succeed in His business. He is able!

See the Picture within the Picture

Even though he was already in his eighties, Joshua fought giants, took possession of their land, and succeeded by God's hand. He knew that God was with him. He was a man who wouldn't turn back.

Joshua reminds me of a cartoon that I saw in a friend's office. A bullfrog in a pond was being swallowed by a crane. The frog's head was already in the crane's mouth. However, the frog's hands had a death grip around the crane's neck. Underneath was the caption, "Never give up!"

God knows the plan that He has for you—it is a good plan that includes life to the fullest. He may lead you into a new season or call you to a new work. He knows how to bring the reality of *who* He created you to be together with *what* He created you to do. It is always time to trust Him, even when the world might count you down. It's never time to quit until God says it's time to stop.

When we look through God's viewfinder, we get the right perspective on life and its difficulties.

> These hard times are small potatoes compared to the coming good times, the lavish celebration prepared for us. There's far more here than meets the eye. The things we see now are here today, gone tomorrow. But the things we can't see now will last forever. (2 Cor. 4:17–18 Message)

When our sight moves beyond the temporal into the eternal—that's the picture within the picture. Faith then moves us to take possession of what we see. Real faith goes the distance and never quits following God.

... Taking the **Next Step** ....

God told Joshua to be strong and courageous. He had to take possession of the Promised Land. In the same way we will have to fight the good fight of faith to rely on what God has promised. The enemy will try to make us give up. Instead, we can be courageous, defeat the giants, and take hold of what Christ has promised us.

Think about It

1. In what ways have people influenced your trust in God—for good or bad?
2. In what ways do you influence the faith of other people?

3. Has there been a critical time in your life when you were tempted to give up but didn't? If so, what were the benefits of not quitting?

4. When has God given you courage to follow Him when you felt like turning back?

5. Think of a time when you stood in faith and God helped you through a major difficulty. In what ways did you experience Him during that time?

Put It into Action

Read Joshua 1:8–9. In what ways do these verses apply to your life? If you haven't already, memorize these verses to strengthen your courage. This week, how can you apply them in your life?

10

Never Give Up on God

Believing God When the Road Is Long

. . . .

> "For I know the plans I have for you," declares the LORD, "plans to prosper you and not to harm you, plans to give you hope and a future."
>
> Jeremiah 29:11 NIV

Several years ago the popular movie *As Good As It Gets* captured the way we sometimes feel when life slams into our hope. The main character is an over-the-top neurotic whose fears get the best of him. One day, while walking through the waiting room of his psychiatrist's office, he looks at the sad sight of the broken people seated around him. Then he asks the question most of us have asked at some point: "What if this is as good as it gets?"

We've all wondered if we might have to struggle with "this issue" or "that person" for the rest of our lives. What if this *is* as good as it gets? That kind of tension pulls against the grain of our faith.

Most of us grew up hearing the familiar words, "Now, don't get your hopes up." We often heard the phrase from well-meaning parents who wanted to protect us from disappointment. At times the warnings were warranted. However, some people learn the lesson so well that they live in a constant state of lowered expectations. Too often we fear getting our hopes up because we've been disappointed so many times.

While we were young, our hope may have been buoyant with expectations. We believed and expected that things would always get better. We hoped for the "happily ever after" endings. For other people, however, hope has always been in short supply. Either way, we all eventually learned that we couldn't always have our way or get what we wanted.

Life has a way of battering even the strongest people. King David was a man who knew the extremes of great joy and enormous disappointment. He won huge victories over formidable enemies. God promoted him from leading sheep to being the king of Israel. But David also experienced the fierce vengeance of the enemy, extreme loss, rejection, grief, fear, moral failure, and anguish of the soul.

When hope looked dim, David wrote some of the most powerful words of confidence in God. He was a man who understood despair. He knew what it felt like to be forgotten: "I am forgotten as a dead man, out of mind; I am like a broken vessel" (Ps. 31:12). He understood feelings of agony: "My heart is in anguish within me, and the terrors of death have fallen upon me" (Ps. 55:4). There were times when he felt like God had forsaken him; his words were mere groanings and he could not find rest (Ps. 22:1–2). At one point the people closest to him distanced themselves, his enemies wanted to destroy him, and the weight of his sin pulled at his soul (Ps. 38).

Through it all David continually cried out to God and trusted Him. It was David who penned these words: "For I hope in You, O Lord; You will answer, O Lord my God"

(Ps. 38:15). We want to hope in God like David did. He kept trusting God, regardless of conditions. Even when life is at its lowest point, we will never have a reason to give up on God.

When we think that we have every reason to be hopeless, we need to stop reasoning and do what David did—start praying! Our hope will never rest secure if it is anchored in this world. God offers a real hope that doesn't shift with circumstances. A hope that knows when life is at its hardest God is always greater. Today God wants to strengthen your hope for the road ahead.

> Now may the God of hope fill you with all joy and peace in believing, so that you will abound in hope by the power of the Holy Spirit. (Rom. 15:13)

As a friend of mine once said, "Jesus is the hope bringer!" He understands what you are going through. He knows the responsibilities, disappointments, and heavy places in your life. He wants to fill you up with joy and peace as you keep your confidence in Him. That's the place where overflowing hope will spring up supernaturally by His Spirit. That kind of joy, peace, and hope is anchored in *believing* Him.

David took all the weights that were pulling him down and brought them straight to God. When his life was in a big mess, he reaffirmed and declared his confidence in God. That kind of hope doesn't come from feelings. It comes from knowing the one who is greater than our broken lives and dreams. He is the one who knows how to hold the universe in order and work all things in our lives for ultimate good. Jesus knows how to turn our messes into His masterpieces. As long as we have breath, we have hope in God.

God's Got the Plan

Have you ever had a day where you looked toward the future and it felt like a giant black hole? When I was having one of those days, I went to lunch with Terri, my friend from college, who fearlessly trusts God. After a long talk, we were headed back to our offices. Terri turned to me and said, "Nancy, don't you know that God *knows* the plan He has for you, a plan to prosper you and not harm you, to give you hope and a future? It's a *known* plan!" I had heard that verse many times; however, when Terri said it's a *known* plan I understood it at a whole new level.

My friend's reminder of God's Word marked my heart with hope. God never sets us adrift, leaving us out on the waters alone. He is always with us. He has a known plan that includes room for us to have preferences and make choices. He says, "Do not fear, for I have redeemed you" (Isa. 43:1). The One who loves us most will never be caught off guard without a plan for us.

There's a story in the Bible that tells of a time when God's people were in dark circumstances. They were in exile, held captive in the foreign land of Babylon. During this time, God sent them hope through the prophet Jeremiah.

> "For I know the plans I have for you," declares the LORD, "plans to prosper you and not to harm you, plans to give you hope and a future." (Jer. 29:11 NIV)

For years I had quoted this verse without focusing on the context of it in the preceding verses. God's people were in exile in a foreign land because of their continued rebellion against Him. It was a "time out" given by God to help them better know and follow Him.

In the middle of this tough circumstance, God opened a door of hope. He told His people to build houses and plant crops. He told them not to decrease but to multiply. He told them to pray for the land of their captors so that they also would have good welfare.

God's known plan is loaded with hope. Our stories are still unfolding, but when we walk with God, our lives are secure even when the future feels insecure. We don't have to try to figure out or fear the future. That doesn't lessen our responsibility to make wise plans and decisions. It does mean that as we have God at the helm, He helps us navigate the journey. He leads us so our destination and our arrival time fit into His greater plan.

A while back I was talking with a very sharp and capable friend who was on the brink of a major opportunity. She voiced concern that since she was in her fifties, she might be too old to follow her dream. Doubt was blurring her vision of what God seemed to be doing. As we walked and talked, I encouraged her that she was right on time in her life.

When God opens a door for us, He never opens it late. We usually wish that He had opened it a lot sooner, but He knows the perfect time. That doesn't mean we can never miss God. It means if we do miss Him, He always has a way to redeem our mistakes. He knows how to weave everything in our lives so it will fit perfectly with His greater kingdom purpose. He is the God of hope!

Letting Go of the Past

A few years ago, I moved from my house into a condo. Moving is tough—physically and emotionally. One day I was sitting alone in the middle of my dining room, packing boxes. Without expecting it I came across the wedding album with photos of my former husband who had left me. It had been many years since the divorce.

Earlier that year I had received a call telling me that he had died following a lengthy illness. His second marriage had lasted only a few years. Several months before he died, I had written him a note. I wanted things to be as right as they could be between us. He called me, we chatted briefly, and then, in a voice broken with emotion, he said, "Every day of my life I have regretted . . ." Suddenly, someone in the background called for him. He started again and could hardly get the words out for the emotion, "Every day of my life I have regretted . . ." Again the person yelled for him, more loudly this time. He said he had to go and would call back.

Almost everything in me wanted to scream, "Finish what you were about to say!" Instead, before saying good-bye I simply reminded him, "God has forgiven you for everything." He was a man who knew God but had made some major wrong turns that didn't end well. We said good-bye and he never called back.

When I saw those wedding photos, an unexpected wave of emotion slammed into me. I immediately started to tap it down. I didn't want to go there. I had so much to do. God had brought me through healing, and my life was in a good place. I didn't want to worm around in old wounds—or so I thought.

Even though that was all history, I sensed that God was saying, "You need to camp there a minute." I paused and looked at the pictures. All of a sudden the rejection, abandonment, disappointment, and broken dreams erupted to the surface. The pain washed over me like it had happened yesterday. Without thinking, one sentence came out of my mouth: "God, I never finished loving him."

With those words something broke inside of me. I felt a release. I realized that I had a lot more love to give him than he was willing to receive. It was a healing moment. The emotion left as fast as it came. That day God pulled a hidden piece of shrapnel from my soul and replaced it with Himself.

"Moving day" comes to all of us. There are times when God calls us to relinquish the past and embrace the new work that He is doing. It may be a job change, relocation, a child leaving for school, retirement, a death, or any important change in our lives. Letting go of things that have deep meaning in our lives is not easy. However, when we hold on to the past at the expense of the present, a piece of ourselves is held back from God. When we won't let go, we miss what God has for us today. This is the core of what God told His people in Isaiah 43:

> Do not call to mind the former things,
> Or ponder things of the past. (v. 18)

The Bible is not saying we shouldn't look at the past or have memories. It is saying that we must not allow our past to bankrupt our present. God doesn't want us to keep staring at things—either good or bad—that used to be. He has something better for us than being locked into yesterday.

Letting go is a choice. Even when the choice is painfully difficult, God will give you the grace to choose well. He will also give you the power to walk in your decision. You never walk away from the past alone. God is right there with you, leading you forward every step of the way.

If you're struggling with past issues and feel like you are in lockdown, ask God to give you the next step toward His freedom. Ask Him to lead you to the help that you need. Decide to do whatever is necessary for you to receive God's healing grace so you can move on down life's road. It may be focused time with Him in His Word, counseling, a support or recovery group, or some other avenue. He doesn't want you to homestead in the past—no matter how good or bad it was. Releasing the past makes room for real hope to come into your present.

God Is Doing Something New

It's one thing to let go of the past; it's another thing to grab hold of what God is doing today. Right after He told Israel to stop longing for the past, He gave them the opportunity for fresh hope in their future.

> Behold, I will do something new,
> Now it will spring forth;
> Will you not be aware of it?
> I will even make a roadway in the wilderness,
> Rivers in the desert. (Isa. 43:19)

Apparently, God can be building a roadway right under our noses, and it is possible for us to miss His work. He told Israel that now was the time He was launching a new work in their lives. Then He asked them, "Will you not be aware of it?"

Could it be that God is birthing something new in your life today that's right under your nose? Think about it. Is there a door in your life that has closed? Maybe there is a new opportunity in front of you waiting for you to walk into it. Too often we hold on to things that are finished simply because we don't want to let go. Sometimes we think that we are waiting on God. We may even be tempted to give up on God ever answering our prayer, while all along He is waiting for us to see the new thing He is doing. It takes a finely tuned heart to know when we are believing God in faith and when we're standing in the way of what He wants to do.

For several years I co-led a Bible discussion group with friends. When I sensed it was time to step down and let someone else lead, there didn't appear to be anyone to step in, so I agreed to another year. In looking back, I think it would have been better to trust that I had heard God, let it go, and believe that He would provide for the group. When I did finally step down, He brought the perfect person to take my place and had a new work for me to do.

God wants us to live freely and follow Him. He promises that He is making a way for our future. If we are in a wilderness, He prepares an open roadway to take us through. If we are in a desert and life seems dry and hard, God knows how to carve out rivers to bring us living water. Real faith stays awake to what God is doing *now*.

God Never Wastes the Wait

While staying at a friend's condo on the Gulf of Mexico and writing, I got up early one day to go walk on the beach. The morning was shrouded in fog. I grabbed my camera and headed out in hope of finding something to photograph. By the time I got down to the water, the sun was burning through the fog. I walked up to a long pier and took a shot of the sun backlighting the pier. As the waves receded, I caught a shaft of the sun's reflection on the wet sand. The resulting photo surprised me. Although I had taken the picture in color, because of the high contrast and backlighting of the sun, it came out almost totally black and white. It's a dramatic photo that shows the sun burning a path through the dense fog. A friend looked at the shot and said, "That's hope." The name stuck and I titled the photo "Hope."

Hope and faith together enable us to see God through the fog of time, circumstance, and challenge. They enable us to go the distance even when it looks like the color has been drained out of life.

In our waiting seasons, we need to remind ourselves of God's vision for our future. In the Bible, the prophet Habakkuk wondered why God seemed to take so long. He asked Him a question that most of us have asked: "How long, O Lord, will I call for help, and You will not hear?" (Hab. 1:2). We all know that empty feeling when we want God to do something but it seems like He's not listening. God gave these words to Habakkuk. They still serve as an encouragement to you and me.

> Then the Lord answered me and said,
> "Record the vision
> And inscribe it on tablets,
> That the one who reads it may run.
> For the vision is yet for the appointed time;
> It hastens toward the goal and it will not fail.
> Though it tarries, wait for it;
> For it will certainly come, it will not delay." (Hab.
> 2:2–3)

It's important to remember the vision that God has given us and to keep it in front of us. We need to know where we are going with God. However, He works on a divine timeline. While we wait for His appointed time we're tempted to get frustrated. Don't go there. Keep your eyes on God and the vision He has given you. Let him keep the timeline.

Karla Faye Tucker, the first woman executed in the state of Texas in over a century, had a vision for prison reform. While in jail, Karla had an encounter with the living Christ and as a result told the truth at her trial. She spent fourteen years on death row and was passionate for the things of God. Like Paul, her love for God and her joy affected inmates and staff alike. Consequently, "death row" had a name change. It became known as "life row." Broken people came and received prayer in this holy place. My close friend, author Linda Strom, discipled Karla for eleven of those years on life row. One time Linda took me with her to meet Karla. I had never met anyone who exuded such a powerful presence of Christ.

In one of Linda's visits, Karla shared her vision of having dorms where inmates could be taught biblical keys for purposeful living. This would happen during their nonworking hours and participants would be held accountable for their studies. Upon release they would have the tools to live life with new hope. Linda told me that Karla wrote her vision down on paper and shared it with a key official in the Texas criminal justice system. That was on February 2, 1998, at 7:30 p.m. Less than twenty-four hours later, Karla received the lethal injection and departed with the words, "I'm going to be with Jesus now."

Today, Karla's dream has come true, as "faith dorms" are being launched throughout the Texas state prison system. The drastic drop in the recidivism rate of the dorm "graduates" is evidence of the power of God's Word. Karla didn't see the fulfillment of what she hoped for while on earth. However, fourteen years after Karla went to be with the Lord, Linda Strom and her team launched another faith dorm. This one was only yards away from life row where Karla first shared her dream with Linda. I taught there last month. Only God! We can be sure that God never wastes the wait in our lives.

Faith Looks to the Future

The day I resigned from my career in business, I felt like the earth shifted under my soul. My position had been restructured again. While I would have kept the same salary with the new position, the new job didn't remotely interest me. For years I had sensed God leading me into full-time ministry and had been praying for His timing. It had been two years since I had become single again. I knew God's timing was just as important as His calling. The moment had finally arrived.

To leave the corporate world, I had to loosen my grip off of a cushy salary, generous benefits, and so-called security. When the company president learned I had resigned, he asked me to meet with him. He asked if I wanted another position in a different department. I said no. I wasn't making a strategic career move; I was going into full-time ministry. That day I didn't know where I was going or how I would get there. But I sensed that God had called me out of the boat to come follow Him.

There are times in our lives when nothing less than faith in God can get the job done. It may be a great opportunity, a life challenge, or a walk on the sheer edge of the unknown with God. These are the times when our faith can take flight and carry us on the white-knuckle adventure of our lives!

When God told Abraham to leave his home, his family, and the life he had known, the Bible says,

> By faith Abraham, when he was called, obeyed by going out to a place which he was to receive for an inheritance; and he went out, not knowing where he was going. (Heb. 11:8)

When the time comes and God calls us to stretch out our faith, we can do what Abraham did—obey! Abraham knew God. He heard Him; he trusted Him; He followed him. This level of faith is not reserved for just the big decisions of life. We are called to live every day by faith.

Faith trusts in God as it focuses on the future. It isn't looking at all the reasons something is impossible. It is focused on the One with whom all things *are* possible.

Faith isn't presuming upon God or assuming or hoping that something will happen. Faith *knows* that what it hopes for is already a done deal in the spiritual realm. Faith is hope that has graduated!

> Now faith is the assurance of things hoped for, the conviction of things not seen. (Heb. 11:1)

Real faith *knows* that God has answered what it hopes for. Anything less is hoping and wishing. Because Abraham was certain that God's promise was already answered, he believed Him right through to the finish line. He saw with his spiritual eyes what his physical eyes could not see—God's promises being fulfilled in the future.

God had told Abraham that he would be the father of many nations through a child with Sarah. He was almost a century old, but still there was no baby. However, even when life didn't make sense, he looked to God.

> In hope against hope he believed. . . . Without becoming weak in faith he contemplated his own body, now as good as dead since he was about a hundred years old, and the deadness of Sarah's womb; yet, with respect to the promise of God, he did not waver in unbelief but grew strong in faith, giving glory to God, and being fully assured that what God had promised, He was able also to perform. (Rom. 4:18–21)

Even a dead womb couldn't slow this guy's faith—because his faith was in God, not in his circumstances.

Maybe circumstances have almost knocked the hope right out of you. Get your hope up! It's the launching pad for your faith. You don't have to waffle around in unbelief. Maybe you're like me in that sometimes my faith is a little anemic. It needs a power boost. At those times we can pray, "I do believe;

help my unbelief" (Mark 9:24). Put your focus back on Jesus, "the author and perfecter of faith" (Heb. 12:2). He gave you faith and He will help your faith grow through His Word.

Faith doesn't mean having all the answers. It means that you are trusting in the only One who *does* have the answers. He knows how to lead you from today into all of His promises. He loves you. Stick tight to Him and "learn the unforced rhythms of grace" (Matt. 11:29 Message).

Keep Your Focus on Jesus

Several years ago I was teaching at a week-long conference while grappling with some challenges in my life. In between sessions I spent extensive time seeking God. The night before I finished teaching, I privately prayed, asking Him to confirm two things: His *vision* and the *confidence* to move forward.

While at the conference, I met a woman named Sandy. She had been a respected part of the group for many years and knew God well. She had a disability that also affected her speech. I had to listen very closely to understand what she was saying. But when she spoke, it was worth the extra effort.

The last morning of the conference, Sandy came up to me just before I was to speak. Through her speech impediment she said, "When I was in the bookstore yesterday, the Lord told me to get these for you." She then placed two small objects in my hand. To be totally honest, red flags automatically fly up in my mind when I hear someone say "The Lord told me . . ."

I looked and Sandy had put two small refrigerator magnets in my hand. *Great*, I thought. *I'm wondering what to do with the rest of my life, and God "told her" to give me refrigerator magnets.* I smiled and politely thanked her.

Then I looked closer, and each magnet had one word written on it. One said *Vision* and the other said *Confidence*. I looked at Sandy, a little shocked, and said, "I really do believe the Lord told you to give these to me." She looked at me, a

Thriving

little shocked, and said, "I know! I told you God told me to give those to you. That's why I bought them!"

Years later, those magnets are still on my refrigerator and are still speaking faith to me. I didn't make any decisions based on them. However, they were and continue to be a great encouragement. They remind me to keep my eyes on Jesus, not on my circumstances—and to never give up on God.

Maybe you're like me and in the tough times you're tempted to wonder if you've really heard God correctly. You wonder if you're on the right track, and if so, why the train isn't moving faster. We will have a lot of opportunities to question if we really heard God, to second-guess if we're going in the right direction, and to wonder why He hasn't done what we wanted Him to do. Regardless of what happens or doesn't happen, never give up on God.

Living in His Greater Purpose

We will see God answer needs before we realize we have them. We will see Him do things that defy the realm of our understanding. We will get the mercy that we need every time we ask for it and even so many times when we don't ask. We will be forgiven more times than we could ever count. We will be blessed beyond anything we could possibly merit. We will be loved by Him unconditionally, and His love will complete us.

As we walk with God, we can learn to become better receivers of all He has given us. We can learn to release His goodness to serve other people. We can pass the blessings that He has given to us on to other people so they can know Him better. In doing so, we become His hands and feet to a broken world. As we do, something amazing happens in *our* lives—*thriving*, that place where we experience life to the fullest in Christ.

Don't get sidetracked into thinking that thriving in life is about figuring out which way to go, what to do, what not to do, getting what we want, avoiding pain, or gathering more

180

goods. It isn't. Life is about knowing God better, loving Him more, and serving to make Him known. That's where faith lives, life flourishes, and fruit grows.

The abundant life in Christ isn't just to make us more comfortable. It is daily living in Him for His greater purpose. Jesus came to serve, not to be served. He came to seek and to save that which was lost. He came to make disciples. He told His followers, "As the Father has sent me, I am sending you" (John 20:21 NIV). Life at its best begins and continues in saying *yes* to Jesus's invitation to, "Come, follow me" (Matt. 4:19 NIV). It's the adventure God has written for you that will make your life count for all of eternity. Now that's as good as it gets!

Taking the **Next Step**

Waiting on God's timing can be challenging. It's important during these periods to keep our focus on Him and what He is doing and to never give up on God! To help encourage us to wait well, He tells us to let go of the past, see the new work that He's doing today, and keep our vision in the forefront. Knowing how to experience Him as we follow His guidance is foundational to thriving in life.

Think about It

1. In what ways does a vision help encourage hope in your life?
2. Think of a specific time when you needed to let go of the past. How did your response help or hinder you with moving forward in your life?
3. Think of a specific time when God began a new work in your life. In what ways did you recognize and embrace the change?

4. In looking back, in what specific ways have you benefited from waiting on God and His timing?
5. In what ways have you experienced closeness with God while waiting?

Put It into Action

If you sense that God has put a vision in your heart, either small or large, write it down and spend time talking with Him about the vision. If not, ask Him to give you His vision for you.

Notes

Chapter 1 A Big Enough Love

1. Andrew Murray, *Absolute Surrender* (Chicago: Moody Press, 1895), 22.
2. A. W. Tozer, *The Knowledge of the Holy* (New York: Harper Collins, 1961), 98.

Chapter 2 The Goodness of God

1. Philip Yancey, *Disappointment with God* (Grand Rapids: Zondervan, 1992), 197.
2. Ruth Paxson, *Life on the Highest Plane: God's Plan for Spiritual Maturity* (Grand Rapids: Kregel, 1996), 39.
3. Tozer, *The Knowledge of the Holy*, 82.

Chapter 3 You Are Here . . . and So Is God

1. A. W. Tozer, *The Pursuit of God* (Harrisburg, PA: Christian Publications, 1993), 62.
2. Ibid., 34.

Chapter 4 Change Your Mind and Change Your Life

1. A number of Bible versions are available for download at https://www.youversion.com/mobile.
2. The McCheyne reading plan is available at https://www.youversion.com/reading-plans/24-mcheyne-one-year-reading-plan.
3. Two helpful websites with study tools are http://www.biblegateway.com and http://www.studylight.org.
4. Tozer, *The Pursuit of God*, 10.

Chapter 7 Great Expectations

1. Richard Foster, *Celebration of Discipline* (New York: HarperOne, 1988), 55.
2. Ibid.

Nancy Grisham (MA, Wheaton College; PhD, Trinity Evangelical Divinity School) launched the speaking ministry Livin' Ignited (www.livinignited.org) in 2004 and speaks at churches, conferences, and special events. She has been a frequent teacher at Willow Creek Community Church's midweek classes and was previously a faculty member at Wheaton College. She lives near Denver, Colorado.

Livin' Ignited

Experiencing Life to the Fullest

Nancy Grisham's speaking ministry—Livin' Ignited—is focused on helping ordinary Christians experience life to the fullest through Christ. In other words, she helps them

THRIVE!

Invite Nancy to speak at your church or next event:

- *Weekend Church Services*
- *Conferences or Retreats*
- *Women's Ministries Gatherings*
- *Evangelism Training*
- *Outreach Events or Equipping*

Visit LivinIgnited.org to watch videos, read testimonials of people impacted by Livin' Ignited, and connect with Nancy.

You can also follow Nancy on **Twitter** at @NancyGrisham or on **Facebook** at Livin' Ignited with Nancy Grisham.